PRAISE FOR

# Life with McDuff
## Lessons Learned from a Therapy Dog

Think *Marley & Me,* but with an intelligent dog!
> — GREGORY A. KOMPES
> Patchwork Path Co-Founder

Through this heart-warming tribute to an extraordinary therapy dog, McFadden skillfully touches our emotions. We share her laughter and feel her grief as she takes us on a journey to learn about the profound impact a dog can have on our lives.
> — MARY R. BURCH, PhD
> AKC Canine Good Citizen Director

*Life with McDuff: Lessons Learned from a Therapy Dog* is a beautiful story about a truly amazing animal. You'll laugh, you'll cry, and you'll marvel at this small but mighty canine hero. With an uncanny intuition, charm and wisdom beyond most of our four-legged friends, McDuff gives us a positive perspective for life.
> — FLORICA HAGENDORN
> Henderson Libraries
> Reading with Rover Coordinator

Judy McFadden quickly acquaints her audience with McDuff's seraphic spirit, then releases the reader on a touching journey that tugs at the collective heartstring. The stories are poignant as the author allows us to be part of the serendipitous encounters between very special people in the Opportunity Village PRIDE Program and this most special dog.
> — LONNA BURRESS, RN
> Chief Officer for Health and Wellness
> Opportunity Village, Inc.

An emotional and titillating journey of rare devotion and kinship. Judy's relationship with McDuff will lead its readers to discover a new type of soulmate … the furry, four-legged kind.
> — DENISE FORANT
> Manager of Volunteer Services
> St. Rose Dominican Hospitals – Rose de Lima Campus

# Life with McDuff

**Lessons Learned
from a
Therapy Dog**

## Judy McFadden

Editors: Gregory Kompes, David Knight, Leslie Hoffman
Designer: Sue Campbell
Cover photos: Lifetouch Church Directories and Portraits

Library of Congress Control Number: 2009927047
ISBN-10: 0-982455-40-2
ISBN-13: 978-0982455-401

The poem, "No Other Way" by Martha Smock is used with permission of Unity, www.unity.org.

Published by:

Summit Mountain Publishing
PO Box 91528
Henderson, Nevada 89009-1528
www.lifewithmcduff.com

Printed in the United States of America
Printed on acid-free paper.

# Dedication

*To my son, Kelly, my rock and my best friend,
and McDuff, the amazing therapy dog
that changed my life and the lives of many others.*

# Contents

# Acknowledgments

**W**HEN I TOLD MY LONG-TIME FRIENDS FROM THE LAW FIRM OF VORYS, Sater, Seymour and Pease that I intended to write a book about McDuff, not one of them exclaimed, "But, you don't know how to write a book." I am grateful and eternally thankful for the faith in me and the encouragement supplied by Dolores Richmond, Vanessa Armstrong, Jill Akermann, Eleanor Meekins, Carol Barber, and Madonna Hood, and for Jan (Accu-Jan) Bryant's unwavering and constant support during the writing and publication of this book.

My sincerest thanks to dear friend Linda Peck who accompanied me at the start of my journey with eight-week-old McDuff. My deepest gratitude to David Knight who edited the book with laughter, tears, and lots of revising. Heartfelt thanks to Owen Porterfield who graciously consented to read my fledgling writing endeavors. They read, edited, and spurred me on from beginning to end and took friendship above and beyond the call of duty. Arby Hambric lifted my spirits and inspired me throughout. Michiko Samad's friendship lightened the burden during the writing process.

My former colleagues at the County Clerk's Office at the Regional Justice Center in Las Vegas; Nancy Noble, Alan Castle, Kathy Kline, Jennifer Kimmel, Jennifer Lott, Jeanette Singer, Aiko Kuwahara, and Linda Smith have kept in touch and cheered me on after I resigned to write the book about McDuff. They have my heartfelt thanks.

My undying gratitude to members of the Henderson Writers' Group who tolerated the beginning stages of my writing during weekly critique sessions. They are dedicated writers who generously and unselfishly offered their expertise and experience.

Through Florica Hagendorn, Reading with Rover Coordinator at the Paseo Verde Library, I met Susan Levanduski and her son, Steven. McDuff brought us together, and I am eternally grateful for their friendship and assistance.

Special thanks to the St. Rose Dominican Hospitals, Siena Campus, volunteers Jean Duncan, Violet Hawkes, Jodi Sieber, Dee Parvin, and Andrea Lubig who never ceased to encourage and support me throughout the book-writing process. My gratitude to my young friends and fellow volunteers Amaan and Adam Shafi, Erik and Ryan Manthei, and Angiela Kivakumar who read chapters and provided their youthful views, and to the Gift Shop ladies, Julie Cain and Mary Shannon.

My sincere appreciation and thanks to the following for their contributions to the book:

Editors Greg Kompes and Leslie Hoffman for their work editing the manuscript; Jerry Simmons who provided hours of advice about publishing and self-publishing; Sue Campbell, the graphic designer who brought McDuff's eyes to life on the book cover; and Ursula Kempe and Mary Burch who offered counsel about the Therapy Dogs International and the AKC Canine Good Citizen® programs.

My love and indebtedness to the following special people in my life: Grover Baird, a father figure who knew my family before my birth and heaped tons of encouragement; Marie Parks, the sister I never had, for believing in this book from the beginning; Mel McFadden, who has been a part of my life for so many years; Cousin Jimmy Gibson, whom I was blessed to discover late in my life. And, my dear son, Kelly McFadden, whose love, belief in me, and constant words of encouragement and support inspired me throughout the entire process. He is my rock and best friend.

Although I cannot thank each person by name, I am particularly grateful to everyone mentioned in the book. I also thank all those who read chapters and provided positive feedback. They know who they are and how grateful I am to them.

And finally, my dear friend Trudy Knight, who I know is looking down from above with a smile on her lips, slowly shaking her head, and saying, "Only Judy."

Faith in a higher power, my son, good friends, and a noble, stubborn, hilarious Scottish terrier carried me through the turbulent times. I know the lessons McDuff taught me while I endured will resonate with readers around the world.

# CHAPTER 1

# Spirit Dog Beginning

*In the beginning of all things, wisdom and
knowledge were with the animals, for Tirawa,
the One Above, did not speak directly to man.
He sent certain animals to tell men he showed
himself through the beast, and that from them,
and from the stars, and the sun, and moon
should man learn...*
—EAGLE CHIEF (LETAKOS-LESA) PAWNEE

THE MOUTHWATERING SMELL OF ROASTING TURKEY MINGLING WITH THE
scent of pine drifted throughout the house. Lights from
the Christmas tree danced on the presents stacked beneath
it. Fire snapped and crackled on the logs burning in the fireplace. A puppy added to the magic on that Christmas day in
Columbus, Ohio.

All eyes focused on the eight-week-old, black Scottish terrier
bundle of energy as he scampered across the floor. The only
danger to him at the time was the oversized, scotch-plaid bow
tied around his neck that kept tripping him. One week later I
literally held his life in the palms of my hands.

The hustle and bustle of the holiday season ended New
Year's Day, 1995 when I dismantled the Christmas tree and
packed away the decorations. My constant worry that McDuff
might swallow or choke on something disappeared. I offered
him a tiny, bone-shaped puppy biscuit. He snatched it from

my fingers, turned, and dashed away. A few seconds later, he rolled on the floor twitching and jerking. *What the heck is going on?* I thought.

Rushing over, I bent down and scooped him up. He continued to twitch and shake in my hands as he tried with all his might to breathe. I scanned the floor for the puppy biscuit and didn't see it anywhere. Probing into his mouth, then down his throat, my fingertip touched it lodged sideways in his windpipe.

"Call the vet!" I screamed to my husband out of sheer panic. As soon as the words left my mouth, their futility dawned on me. If it remained there much longer, my tiny bundle of joy would suffocate from lack of air.

A strange calm descended over me. I grabbed his hind legs and shook him upside down in an attempt to dislodge the biscuit. No luck; the convulsions worsened. With trembling hands, I turned him over onto his back, facing me, and balanced him on my palms.

Holding him around his tiny body, I began applying the Heimlich maneuver, pushing in with my thumbs just below his rib cage. After about three compressions, I heard a dull thud. McDuff became deathly still. His small chest quivered, raised and moved — he began to breathe again.

I reached into his mouth and located the object stuck to the roof. It had propelled forth with such force that I had to pry it out with my finger. Dropping down on my knees, weak and shaking, I hugged his quivering body to my face. Tears of relief streamed down my cheeks when I realized how close I had come to losing him.

Although I didn't know it at the time, I saved McDuff's life because we were meant to travel together. He had a mission to complete on earth, and I believed it was my destiny to accompany him on that unforgettable, glorious journey.

McDuff became my teacher, companion, and a source of emotional support through the most trying years of my life. I witnessed the healing, comfort, and joy he dispensed, and his supernatural ability to connect with people and animals.

Most important of all, he taught me invaluable lessons about life along the way. And he didn't stop — even after his death.

McDuff's mystical abilities became obvious to me the day I picked him up from the kennel. I had decided to rekindle my childhood connection with dogs by giving my husband a puppy for Christmas. At least, that's the excuse I gave to get my hands on one.

All went well in the marriage for a while, but things deteriorated drastically. For now, my goal was to find my spouse the most suitable canine companion. After considerable research on breeds, I zeroed in on Scottish terriers.

Despite the intense exploration, the deciding factor boiled down to my grandmother's set of red glasses with images of black Scottish terriers around the rims. I'd admired them since childhood. Yes, I know that's not a scientific reason for selecting a dog, but science goes only so far when choosing man's best friend.

The next job was to find a kennel in my area that sold Scotties. I told my good friend, Trudy, that I wanted to buy a Scottish terrier puppy. She lived about nine miles south of Columbus in Grove City.

"Jude, you're in luck. There's a kennel close to me that specializes in breeding Scotties."

I called Debcha Kennels and talked to Orville, the owner.

"A new litter of puppies will be ready to go by Christmas. Come down in a few weeks and look them over."

I tingled with excitement on the day I drove to the kennel. I liked Orville the moment I saw him. He told me all about the litter's parents and brought mom and dad out so I could meet them. After that, he introduced me to four black balls of fluff on legs. To my amazement, they looked exactly alike. How in the world could anyone tell them apart?

Orville carefully deposited each puppy into a wire cage through an opening in the top. When I put my hand in, all the puppies tumbled over each other to lick and smell it. They jumped and bounded in every direction, but kept running back to my wiggling fingers. However, it didn't take them long to lose interest — except for one. He focused on my fingers and refused to go away. I felt an instant bond. Something clicked between us. I turned to Orville and said, "I want this one."

A problem existed. He informed me that another lady had first pick of the litter and would be by in a few days to choose one of the puppies. My heart sank.

*Oh, no,* I thought, *he's the one I want; none of the others will do.*

Orville read the disappointment on my face.

"I've got an idea, Judy. His ears aren't standing up yet. I'll point that out to the lady, and it might discourage her from choosing him. Scotties' ears are down when they are first born, but within weeks stand up on their own. Some lag behind others," he explained.

To address the problem of them all looking alike, he came up with another great plan. "In case his ears come up before she gets here, I'll distinguish him in some way."

Orville took a black felt marker, turned the struggling puppy over, and drew circles around his nipples. If the lady chose the one with the exotic teats, I was out of luck. All I could do was wait to see what happened. On Christmas Eve, I got the best present ever.

"You can come and pick up your puppy," Orville said with a chuckle over the phone.

I called my friend, Linda, who had offered to ride with me to hold him while I drove home, and told her the good news. The first of many mysterious occurrences in my life with McDuff happened on that day.

After paying Orville, I picked McDuff up and held him upright to face me at about eye level. While supporting his rear end on the palm of my left hand, with my right hand under his two front paws, I saw two smoldering dark eyes burning into mine like a flame. Years later I became familiar with that stare, especially in his therapy dog work.

That little creature held my gaze for what seemed like ages. It was as though he peered into my very soul. Then, the thought, *I wonder what adventures we two are going to have together,* came into my mind. The thought wasn't strange. What was strange is that it didn't come from me. It came to me from him. Chills and a weird sensation ran down my spine. I put him down — fast. Shaking it off, I decided not to mention it to anyone afraid they would question my sanity. Still, I wondered about it. Looking back now, I know it foretold of things to come.

Native Americans believe in spirit animals, or totems, endowed with special powers. They accompany an individual acting as a spiritual guide both in the physical and spiritual world. These spirit animals offer power and wisdom throughout a lifetime to the individuals who communicate with them.

Many cultures share a similar belief. The Shaman consults spirits of animals to learn and acquire wisdom from them. In case you think the spirit animal concept is outside our culture, think again. Other Americans have totems, too.

Social clubs like the Benevolent and Protective Order of Elks, Loyal Order of Moose, and Lions Club embrace totems. Sports fans are exposed to numerous displays of power animals.

Football fans have Lions, Panthers, and Jaguars. Basketball fans cheer Bulls, Bucks, and Bobcats. We can't leave baseball fans out, because they root for Cardinals, Orioles, and Blue Jays. Even Christianity is represented by two totems, the fish and the lamb.

When my son, Kelly, was a toddler, his totem was a stuffed brown bear. He adored Teddy and slept with him every night for years. But, how could I, a coal miner's daughter running through the rolling hills of southwestern Pennsylvania with her beloved dogs, know about totems? I didn't know then that one day a spirit dog would enter into and change my life.

A connection existed to Native Americans in my ancestry. My maternal great-grandmother's mother was a member of the Chippewa tribe. Once, at an Indian Pow Wow, a woman stared at me for a while and exclaimed, "You belong to the Wolf clan." There are nine animals that act as spiritual guides, and one of them is the wolf. Dogs are descended from wolves.

A keen awareness for animals of all kinds existed in me from childhood. On walks through the woods, I always knew where wild things hid. My young playmates stood by in awe while I pointed out the camouflaged rabbit under a bush, or the bird nest concealed among tree branches. Watching a hummingbird nest I discovered during one of my solitary expeditions afforded hours of secret pleasure.

I tamed and rode bareback the half-wild horses that were used to work in the coal mines. Fish on stringers from my father's fishing trips were kept alive in our kitchen sink by the water I secretly poured over them.

I felt and still feel a kinship with all animals, but dogs held a special place in my heart. Butch exemplified my unique connection with them.

All the coal mining families living in the weather-worn, wooden company houses at Beeson Works knew about my extraordinary bond with dogs. Many times a neighbor dashed across our concrete front porch and pounded on my parent's door.

"Mrs. Jones, Butch is loose again. Get Judy!"

"Judy," my mother called in a voice shrill with anxiety, "find Butch and keep him out of the patch until Miss Louise gets home from work."

Butch, a big, long-haired, black and brown dog, belonged to a family friend who lived across the road. Keeping him chained to an iron stake in the ground year round didn't help his notoriously bad temperament.

Most dogs in Beeson were mixed breeds, but you could tell from the looks of him that a German shepherd lurked somewhere in his family tree. No one could get near him except his owner — and me.

It didn't take long to find Butch. All I did was follow the trail of maimed and dead dogs leading to him. He had a special fondness for killing puppies. Once, I saw him grab a helpless puppy in his mouth, shake it ferociously from side to side, and fling it high up in the air. The poor thing died before it hit the ground.

Butch never attacked a human. Probably because word of his escape sent panic-stricken people streaking to the safety of their homes where they remained until I caught him.

"Come here, Butch!" I ordered when I had him in sight. After a thorough scolding, he cowered down before me. I led him away by the piece of dangling chain into the nearby woods, leaving the carnage behind. Some sight — a skinny, pigtailed schoolgirl protecting the neighborhood from a blood-soaked, canine killing machine.

Butch and I exited the woods later in the day to await Miss Louise's arrival from work. As she approached, she saw us sitting on her front porch, observed the broken chain by his doghouse, and immediately figured out what happened.

"Judy, did he kill any dogs or hurt anybody this time?" she asked, fearing the worst.

"He killed one dog and some puppies, but no people were hurt."

Miss Louise jerked Butch by the broken chain and banished him to the cellar under her house. I watched her stomp off to find a bigger, heavier chain to contain him. But, from past experience, we knew Butch would break it eventually and terrorize the neighborhood again.

Maybe my childhood connection with Butch was an indication of my mysterious relationship with dogs, and why McDuff chose me to accompany him on his mission. He was right about the adventures we would experience together. They commenced at obedience school. The extraordinary ability he exhibited throughout his life surfaced on graduation night, along with the pride and frustration I would feel on my journey with him down through the years.

### CHAPTER 2

# Obedience Class Valedictorian

*Life is but one continual course of instruction.*
—ROWLAND HILL

"**M**CDUFF IS GRADUATING!" THE NOVEMBER 4, 1998 INVITATIONS invited my friends to witness the happy event and enjoy refreshments provided for the occasion. Graduation is recognized by all as a time of happiness and exhilaration. McDuff's rite of passage from obedience school turned into one of the most nerve-wracking and humiliating nights of my life.

Two things jumped out many times during my research on Scottish terriers; their intelligence and their stubbornness. I detected from the beginning McDuff had a mind of his own. While still a young puppy, the strong will of that little mind came out, revealing the first tip of the stubbornness iceberg.

One day I picked him up and held him under his two front legs, facing me, his hind legs dangling underneath him. He looked adorable. After a short while, he figured I'd held him long enough. He started to squirm and twist around.

When I continued to hold him anyway, the squirming and wiggling escalated. I tightened my grip. That's when McDuff threw what can only be described as a canine temper tantrum.

I've never heard such ominous sounds coming out of any animal. He shrieked like a goblin from hell. Such unearthly noises emerging from a tiny puppy floored me. Frightened and caught off guard, I froze on the spot.

He continued, gathering steam and progressively getting louder, twitching and jerking like he didn't have a bone in his body. After getting over my initial fright, I shook him once and said, "No!" He immediately became quiet. His entire body went limp. He hung between my hands swinging like a rag doll, his head flopped over to one side.

*Did I shake him too hard?* I wondered. But, I knew better than that. He dangled in the breeze — no movement, no sound. Carefully lowering him to the floor, I placed him on his side not knowing what to expect. As soon as his body touched the carpet, up he scrambled, and shot off across the floor.

Still shaken up, I called out for my husband and told him about it. He walked over to McDuff, picked him up, and held him the way I'd described. Looking him in the eyes, he said, "No." His body drooped the way it had for me. My husband lowered him to the floor. McDuff popped up and scampered away.

From then on, while he was small enough, we'd pick him up and say "No" to discipline him. He never repeated the bad behavior after that. Remembering what I learned during my research on Scotties, I made up my mind to put him in obedience school at some point.

When McDuff was four years old, I had time to train with him. I enrolled him in Columbus All-Breed Training Club, an obedience school in a rural area on the southeast side of Columbus. The large, khaki green building had a parking lot on one side, and an area for the dogs to exercise and relieve themselves out back.

The first class was held without the dogs. Our instructor explained the rules and provided an overview of the training. She made it clear from the beginning she would not train our dogs for us. We would learn how to do the training. Afterward, we stood around and observed classes in session. I couldn't wait to get started with McDuff the following week.

Class night finally arrived. I hurried home from the law firm of Vorys, Sater, Seymour and Pease where I had worked for years as a legal secretary. Grabbing a quick bite to eat, I cut McDuff's walk short that evening before setting out.

We arrived for the first Wednesday evening class to a smorgasbord of excited dogs with their enthusiastic owners. McDuff pranced and danced around in delight eager to partake in this tempting buffet. But, a big disappointment awaited him.

"You two, with the Scottie and fox terrier, move with your dogs to the back of the room," the blonde, pony tailed, no-nonsense instructor barked. "Don't let them make eye contact with the other dogs."

The fox terrier was going bonkers, lunging and trying to attack every dog in sight. For some reason, he felt a kinship with McDuff and didn't challenge him, perhaps because they were the dreaded "terriers."

McDuff lunged and went bonkers, too, but for an entirely different reason. He wanted to get to each and every one of those dogs in our class to play with them. I gathered up enough nerve to speak out.

"McDuff's not mean. He just wants to play."

The instructor shot me a dirty look and repeated her command for banishment of the terriers. I felt like a leper standing against the back wall watching the class proceed without us. Half way through, McDuff and the fox terrier were permitted to rejoin the class.

"Keep the terriers away from the other dogs, and walk single file around the training area," the instructor ordered.

The fox terrier still rampaged and challenged the other dogs. McDuff, on the other hand, leaped ahead to play with the dog in front of us. When I jerked him back, he dropped behind me to play with the dog behind us. This went on the whole time to my embarrassment and dismay.

After class, the instructor motioned me to remain. *Oh boy, we're in trouble again,* I thought as I watched her approach.

"I owe you an apology," she said.

"Why do you need to apologize to me?"

She showed me a two-inch scar on her right hand between her thumb and forefinger. "I got this from a Scottish terrier when I tried to break up a dog fight. The Scottie attacked a Great Dane in one of my obedience classes," she said. "Oh, he didn't bite me intentionally, but they're well-known for their aggressiveness toward other dogs."

She took a long look at McDuff, shook her head and exclaimed, "I have never seen a Scottish terrier in all my years of training with a temperament like his."

"I tried to tell you he just wanted to play."

"See you next week," she said patting his head before walking away.

I worked with McDuff every chance I got during the week. He caught on to everything super fast, completely different from my experience with my other dogs. He seemed to know what I wanted him to do without my telling him. Down the road I would find out the reason for that. If I could get him to settle down and leave the other dogs alone in class, we'd be set.

The instructor banned the fox terrier from the class when we returned the next week, but she permitted McDuff to remain. Once again, he started his old tricks. So many dogs to fool around with, so little time. How was I going to make him realize this wasn't recess at kindergarten?

The instructor saw my predicament. She came over and showed me how to use his slip chain collar to stop him from trying to play with the other dogs. I learned why the collar was mandatory, because after a couple hard jerks on it with the leash, he got the message. Class became fun after that.

McDuff learned the basic obedience commands to perfection, excelling at everything and performing with style and flair. Anticipating what I wanted him to do, he executed flawlessly. We practiced daily after work and on weekends in a large open field beside a school. McDuff had his romp in the field off leash. Afterward, we practiced obedience commands. We didn't miss a class during the eight weeks before graduation.

The big night arrived. Bubbling with excitement, I hurried home from work. McDuff's progress made me proud, and I couldn't wait to show him off. To make sure he had ample time to "empty" himself, I skipped eating my dinner. I didn't want a mishap to spoil our special night.

We left home in the dark. I stopped on the way at a field nearby to allow McDuff to relieve himself. Usually, I took him to the area by the school, but this evening I wanted to save time and get to class before my guests arrived. After I opened the car door, he jumped out and exploded into the night. I didn't worry that he wouldn't come back when called.

Invisible in the darkness because of his black coat, I tracked him as he roamed about by the jingling of the dog tags on his collar. *I better give him some extra time.* After a while, I called him. He promptly returned and jumped into the back seat.

McDuff rode in the car with his front feet on the armrest between the front seats. His back feet rested on the edge of the rear seat. That way he could look forward out of the windshield. I started up and drove off, eager to see my friends and share McDuff's graduation cake with them.

It wasn't long before a pungent odor drifted throughout the car. It got stronger and stronger, but didn't cause me concern. Probably, the aroma that sometimes emanated from the animal rendering plant on the south side of Columbus. The air in that part of town got raunchy at times.

Rolling down the car window, I took a whiff. To my surprise, it smelled fresh and clean outside. Baffled, I glanced over at McDuff, but saw nothing on him or his front feet.

The closer I got to the obedience school, the more revolting the smell became. In order to get a better look, I pulled the car over to the side of the highway and stopped. Turning on the dome light while still sitting in the driver's seat, I gave McDuff a quick once over.

Although only the side facing me was visible, I detected nothing out of the ordinary. He looked at me and shuffled his front feet anxious to get started. Once more, we started on our way.

By the time we pulled into the parking lot, the stench was unbearable. With a bubbling and churning stomach, I shot out of the car, ran around to the passenger side to open the door. Hooking McDuff's leash onto his collar, I let him out.

When he jumped down to the ground and turned around, I got a good look at the side that faced away from me in the car. I also got the shock of my life. His clean, shiny black coat was smeared with a Hershey-brown substance that extended from his shoulder to his tail.

Feeling like I'd been kicked in the pit of my stomach, I gasped for air. I knew my dog all too well. He never missed a chance to roll in dog or cat poop. Anything dead that he could flop on was a special delight. To make matters worse, I wasn't sure what type of disgusting substances I was dealing with. What had he been exposed to on his nocturnal excursion under the cover of darkness in that field?

I hated to consider it, but from the smell of him, something from a human could be in the concoction. I freaked. Friends would soon arrive, and he reeked enough to singe the hairs in your nostrils. We'd be on full display in front of everyone during the evaluation. There was nowhere to run and no hole deep enough for both of us to hide. *What am I going to do?*

There was nothing for me to do, but go into the building and try to clean him up the best I could. Water bowls sat on the floor inside the building for the dogs to drink from if they got thirsty. I could swipe one of them, grab some paper towels from the ladies room, and do my best to tidy him up.

Believe me, I didn't look forward to this sickening cleanup at all. Where any kind of feces is concerned, my weak stomach rebels big time. Changing my son's diapers had caused me to throw up until I got used to doing it.

I entered the building head down to avoid eye contact or conversation. Taking a deep breath, I glanced around. The place buzzed with the sound of excited dogs and handlers anticipating graduation. Shampooed, fluffed up, perfumed dogs stood by their proud owners. The multi-colored canine standing by my side stunk to high heaven.

All three training rings bustled. Crowds of people swirled on the sidelines, watching. Assuming a low profile, I picked my way through them. As I passed an instructor, her nose twitched and her head snapped around in our direction.

"Folks, be sure to take your dogs outside to the exercise area before your evaluation starts to prevent any accidents," she urgently encouraged the owners standing nearby.

I slunk to the nearest restroom and told McDuff to "Stay." Dashing inside, I grabbed handfuls of paper towels and made a quick exit. Confiscating one of the bowls of water, I found an isolated corner and went to work on the repulsive mixture. *Please, God, don't let me start vomiting now and draw attention to us.* After three or four dry heaves, I began to wipe him off.

Now, McDuff was in deep trouble, and he knew it. He wouldn't look at me and kept turning away, head hung in misery, as I hissed words like daggers through clinched teeth under my breath.

"I could just strangle you." I vacillated between violence, "I'm going to kill you," and self-pity, "Why did you have to do this to me tonight of all nights?"

After a while, dark chocolate brown turned to milk chocolate brown, and black fur played peek-a-boo in between. I didn't have enough time to get all of it off. Friends began arriving. Soon class would begin.

I welcomed my guests with a forced smile, avoiding eye contact as I tried to angle McDuff's streaked side away from them. They laughed and teased me about the graduation invitations and cake. No one mentioned that awful stench. It wasn't easy for me to ignore it, or the Scottie with the funny colored black coat, but I managed.

I believe my friends thought a dog training facility smelled that way because of all of the dogs in the building. They didn't have a clue. Everyone settled down and class began.

McDuff was the second dog to be evaluated. He stared up at me with pleading eyes as we waited for the signal to start. *Please, don't be mad at me. I'm going to make it up to you.* What he got from me in return was an icy, cold glower.

The instructor raised her hand and signaled us to start. Paranoia gripped me as I walked around the ring on legs stiff as two wooden boards. *Is that lady laughing at his strange color? What's that man pointing at? Thank goodness they're too far away to smell him.*

All eyes glued on us as we executed the beginning obedience requirements for graduation. McDuff performed like a champ. He executed every task perfectly. We finished without a hitch. The agonizing wait for evaluation of the class began.

I laughed, chatted, and continued to ignore the fumes coming from my unsavory dog. Owners nervously glanced at theirs. On that crisp autumn night, I noticed an unusual number of them taking dogs outside to the exercise area.

There were two awards to be given along with the Certificate of Completion for successfully completing the beginning obedience course. I dished out cake to my friends and others in the class while waiting for our instructor to tabulate the points.

When she finished, she summoned all of the class over and announced the winner of the trophy and first place blue ribbon.

"The winner of the beginning obedience class trophy is . . . McDuff," the instructor announced. Claps rang out, pats on the back, and praise from my classmates. She waited for us to calm down before continuing.

"The winner of the first place blue ribbon is . . . McDuff."

I was speechless. My stink bomb had swept the field. Everyone rushed over to congratulate me and rave about McDuff's performance. After class, the instructor approached me.

"I gave McDuff the highest score in all my years of training dogs. The only reason I took anything off was because you walked him too fast."

Could it be I wanted to get out of the spotlight and into a hole as fast as possible? I still have the graduation evaluation score sheet with a total score of ninety-nine and one-half points.

All was forgiven that evening. What did it matter that I had to ride home with him stinking worse than a skunk? Did I care that he needed a bath before I could flop my exhausted and emotionally drained body into bed? No, I did not. My dog was valedictorian of the class. McDuff was something special.

# CHAPTER 3

# Scottie with Attitude

*For success, attitude is equally*
*important as ability.*
—HARRY F. BANKS

**S**COTTISH TERRIERS HAVE A PRESENCE UNLIKE ANY OTHER DOG. THE way they walk and look, their independent, stubborn streak and supreme intelligence distinguish them from other canines. I've owned a lot of dogs before, but none like a Scottie. They are a breed apart.

Dignity is a trait often attributed to them. McDuff couldn't stand ridicule. My referring to him in a jeering manner as a "big-headed, fat rat" always elicited a low growl of protest as he turned his back and walked away from me.

He wasn't a lap dog either. Only when he felt like it, and on his own terms, would he jump up and sit on my lap.

McDuff's gait was distinctive and characteristic of the breed. Once you see a Scottie strut by, you won't forget it. Those short legs move in a peculiar way, unlike the square trot or walk you see in breeds with long legs. The front legs don't move parallel. They reach out and come slightly inward because of their deep broad chest.

I thought McDuff had a deformity when he was a puppy because of the way he moved. His legs didn't look or seem to work right. The movement seemed all wrong compared to other dogs I'd owned. But, that didn't matter, because by then,

I was too crazy about him to return him to the kennel and demand my money back.

The way he walked wasn't his only unique characteristic. Scotties have a distinctive look. McDuff's protruding eyebrows and flowing beard, as well as those extra long, erect ears, proved irresistible to the probing fingers of small children.

And, I bet you've seen handlers lift Scotties down from a table to the floor at dog shows, one hand under the chest and by the base of their tail with the other hand. McDuff's tail, broad at the base, tapered up to a point at the tip. Scottish hunters long ago would reach into a hole, grasp the thick part of the tail, and pull the Scottie and prey out of the hole together.

The Scottish terrier breed dates back to the late 1800s. They have two coats: a wiry outercoat, and underneath it a soft undercoat. Scotties come in three basic colors: black, all shades of brindle, and wheaten, a light, golden color.

Males should weigh between nineteen and twenty-two pounds, females between eighteen and twenty-one pounds. McDuff tended to be on the pudgy side.

Their original purpose was to work underground to hunt and kill animals like foxes, badgers, vermin, and rodents. It required a short-legged, low-to-the-ground body to enter dens and burrows. They had to be exceptionally strong, ferocious, and courageous for their underground battles, thus the need for an aggressive temperament.

McDuff differed from the typical Scottie when it came to aggressiveness. He was the Will Rogers of canines; he never met a dog he didn't like — even after his clash with a monster pit bull. He turned his back on his Scottish breeding in another way, too. He loved cats. But, when it came to intelligence, he outshone any dog I've ever seen.

It pains me to admit this, but many times, he outsmarted me. While watching the Westminster Kennel Club Dog Show, I heard an announcer say, "The Scottish terrier is the only breed of dog that knows he is smarter than his master." I found out why.

I became aware of his cunning when he was about four months old. McDuff grabbed my husband's black slipper from under the bed and raced out of the bedroom scrambling down the carpeted stairs into the living room. I took off right behind him.

Chasing after him down the steps, I found him sitting calmly in the middle of the living room floor with the bedroom slipper nowhere in sight. *He couldn't have gone out of the living room. I was right on his heels,* I thought. *Where is it?*

He sat watching, never moving from the spot, as I searched around the room. His head turned, his eyes tracked every move, but his butt remained stuck to the floor. *What's that sticking out from underneath him?*

I picked him up, and guess what I found? The slipper mashed beneath his black rear end and the floor. McDuff sat on it the whole time I searched. I overlooked it since he and the slipper were the same color. Was it a coincidence or did he deliberately sit on that slipper to hide it? I chose at the time to believe coincidence; he couldn't be that smart.

Not long after that, my frowning husband confronted me one morning. "Judy, why do you keep taking my cough drops from the night stand by the bed? You could at least put the wrappers in the trash can instead of throwing them on the floor."

I didn't have the slightest idea what he was talking about and told him so in no uncertain terms. He dropped the subject.

A few days later he brought it up again. I informed him with eyes flashing I had no medical need for his cough drops, and even if I did, I wasn't sloppy enough to throw wrappers on the floor. Boom! The thought hit us at the same time. McDuff? But, he couldn't remove the wrappers.

We decided to bait a trap. Sure enough, we caught him attempting to steal a cough drop. We gave one to him and watched in amazement as he removed the paper and devoured it. No more accusations from my husband or cough drops left on the nightstand after that. We soon discovered his ability to remove coverings didn't end with cough drops.

Our walks with McDuff took us by Mr. Petzinger's house. He and his wife lived in a beautiful red brick house with a glass enclosed front porch. Two bird baths and a bird feeder, along with a feeder for squirrels, adorned the large front yard ablaze with colorful flowers planted by Mrs. Petzinger.

Mr. Petzinger sat in a high-backed, white wooden chair and fed shelled peanuts to the squirrels that gathered at the feeder every day. He and McDuff became great pals, and McDuff joined the squirrel brigade. He sat in front of the chair and waited patiently while Mr. Petzinger shelled and skinned the peanuts, then tossed them to him. It became their daily ritual.

One evening I lounged on my comfortable wing back, living room chair shelling peanuts and sharing them with McDuff. As I got up to leave the room one of them fell to the floor. Before I could reach down and pick it up, McDuff snatched it.

I watched in amazement as he removed the shell in his mouth, and spat it out along with the peanut. Then, he picked up the peanut, expelled the skin onto the rug, and proceeded to devour the naked peanut.

Damp and crinkled, the scorned skin lay on the floor for me to clean up. It happened so fast I couldn't believe my eyes. To be sure it wasn't a fluke, I gave him another one. He did the same thing. McDuff performed that feat many times at nursing homes and hospitals in later years during therapy dog work.

He used his teeth in another way that didn't require as much finesse. His ferocious ancestors used them to catch and kill the most vicious animals. McDuff made good use of those powerful weapons for a purpose other than fighting ferocious burrow animals as he was bred to do. He used them to disembowel and de-squeak stuffed toys.

All pet owners derive pleasure from buying toys for their pets. You know the kind I mean: something soft, cuddly, and cute with a squeaker inside to make tantalizing noise. Cost doesn't matter, because our companions deserve the best.

While still a puppy, I bought him toys and watched, amused, while he pounced on them, shaking his little head and emitting semi-threatening growls. "How cute," I thought as he scurried across the floor in pursuit of one of his stuffed playthings. Then, he grew up and things changed. It got ugly.

I made the mistake of paying ten dollars for a toy. Never again. He destroyed it in a matter of seconds. I witnessed first hand what those daggers could do.

First, he peeled the outer cover like skinning a catfish, and pulled out the white, fluffy stuffing, frantically trying to get to the squeaker inside. Once he had completely gutted the toy and silenced that squeaking sound inside, he had no more use for it. He walked away spitting fluff from his mouth, the demolished wreck tossed away like a worn-out, old shoe.

Ten dollars poorer and shell-shocked, I picked up the silenced squeaker and cleaned up the wads of padding and pieces of cloth scattered across the floor.

Well, it didn't take long for me to start shopping at toy stores in the mall for marked-down stock after that. I'd give them to him and watch him tear them apart the way a buzz saw rips through wood. My son, Kelly, and I timed the destruction. It took him seconds to gut toys.

He failed with one though. While walking through the park, we found a small stuffed lion that a school kid probably dropped. He spent many hours trying to demolish it and get to the squeaker inside without success. He couldn't make a dent in it.

Maybe it fell from an Unidentified Flying Object and was made of materials from outer space. As battered as it is, I keep it in my cedar chest with other sentimental things. When I croak, Kelly won't know what to make of the strange memorabilia he'll find in there.

McDuff also differed from other canines when it came to eye contact. Direct, prolonged eye contact is difficult, if not impossible, for dogs. Try this experiment. Make eye contact with your dog and hold it. Watch its reaction.

It will probably become uncomfortable and look away. Continue to stare and it may even start to yawn, a sign of stress in a dog. Eye contact to a dog is a sign of challenge or confrontation going back to their wolf ancestry. Submissive wolves avoid the eyes of dominant members of the pack.

McDuff wasn't the least bit intimidated by my long stare. Later, I came to discover the looks between us served another purpose. Through them an eerie telepathy transpired. Whatever he was thinking somehow passed on to me. I came to realize it had happened that day at the kennel when I picked him up.

An example of how it worked occurred on our walks in the field by the school when I'd spot a squirrel. He loved to chase squirrels. I'd say, "I see a squirrel, Duff." With no effort on his part to locate the squirrel, his head whipped around, and he stared into my eyes. *Where?*

"Over there," I said, pointing in the direction of the squirrel. His head snapped around in that direction. If he didn't see it at first, he looked back at me. *Are you fooling me?*

"No, Dummy," I'd say, pointing again.

After he spotted the squirrel, he gave me a quick look. *I see it!* And he took off after it like a bullet shot from a gun.

The chase was on. Those squirrels didn't play fair, though. Every time he came close to catching one, it leaped on top of the chain link fence out of his reach which frustrated McDuff to no end.

Our strange communication wasn't always initiated by me. One summer I participated in the neighborhood garage sale, a joyous occasion for McDuff. He welcomed every potential buyer by eagerly greeting them as they walked down the driveway into the garage to check out the goods. His enthusiastic welcome caused my sales to skyrocket that day.

A teenage girl strolled down the street ahead of her mother, saw McDuff, and made a big fuss over him. She turned and yelled back, "Mom, come here and see this adorable Scottie."

When her mother arrived at the driveway, she smiled at the sight of McDuff's approach, clasped her hands in front of her, and exclaimed, "Oh, how cute. Is she pregnant?"

Well, he had a tendency to be on the chunky side, and his thick coat made him appear much wider. After she said that, I swear, McDuff stopped dead in his tracks, whipped his head around, and looked straight at me. *"Can you believe she said that? Is she stupid? What nerve."*

Laughing so hard, I couldn't tell the lady that "she" was a "he." They never figured out what amused me so much, but indignant McDuff knew. I decided to cut back on the treats to save him any further embarrassment. He might have looked like a fertile female to that lady, but she had it all wrong. Scottie testosterone made McDuff fearless.

Noises didn't bother him, which was strange. Scotties' ears are sensitive to sound, because they had to hear mice and rats hiding underground. No trembling and hiding under the bed for him during thunderstorms.

He growled and barked back at the thunder if the rumbling became too fierce. Many times I took him with me to the park on Independence Day to watch the fireworks.

"I can't believe he's not afraid of the noise," countless people walked up and told me. "My dog would be scared out of his wits."

With tears in her eyes, one lady told me how her dog ran away on the Fourth of July after being frightened by fireworks from a nearby park. Only once did McDuff lose his cool because of a loud sound.

Kelly and I went to the park to watch the launching of hot air balloons one sunny afternoon. The many Crayola colored balloons dazzled my eyes. Some were adorned with cartoon characters, intricate artwork, and fancy designs.

Soccer and basketball-shaped balloons scored goals in their sky games. They dotted the cloudless blue sky like candy sprinkles. It's amazing how gigantic they are when viewed up close.

For a long time, we watched as they inflated and lifted off. As we walked across the open field to leave, a balloon hovered overhead. We heard one of the operators in the gondola say, "Look at that Scottie dog down there." They maneuvered the balloon in our direction, close enough for us to shout back and forth about McDuff. He sat beside me off leash taking it all in.

With a deafening, hissing blast of flaming propane, the balloon started to ascend once more. That was too much for McDuff. I think the loud noise combined with the size of the balloon floating over his head spooked him. He took off running like a jackrabbit across the busy street by the park.

Luckily, Kelly ran him down before he got lost or killed by traffic. What a close call. That's the only time he did anything to cause me concern. From what I've read and heard, I bet many dog owners wish they could make that claim.

Many stories tell of the destructiveness of dogs rampaging in a home, how they run amok in fright when left alone during a thunderstorm. Or, how dogs steal food from the kitchen, chew up furniture and shoes, or tear curtains from windows. Not to mention pooping all over the place. My dog never did anything like that. McDuff didn't have time to mess up. He was on a mission and needed to focus on training for his purpose in life.

# CHAPTER 4

# Therapy Dog McDuff

*Find a need and fill it.*
—RUTH STAFFORD PEALE

**A**BLOOD-CURDLING SCREAM PIERCED THE AIR AS I STARTED TO LEAVE the St. Rose Dominican Hospitals, Rose de Lima Campus, emergency room with McDuff. One of the nurses hurried over to stop us from going out the door. "Could you please wait until the doctor finishes stitching a little girl's head? We told her that she could see the doggie if she was a good girl."

Walking to the examination room where the stitches were being administered, I spied into the cubicle. The small child lay on the treatment table surrounded by the nurses and doctor. She looked to be around four-years-old.

A straight jacket-like garment strapped around her body confined and contributed to her terror. For the longest time, her screams rang throughout the emergency room. Finally, the doctor finished, and the nurse removed the restraints. I got a clear look at the curly-haired little girl with the frightened, tear-stained face.

One of the nurses lifted her from the treatment table. Crying softly as her feet touched the floor, her eyes landed on McDuff sitting outside. Like sunshine breaking through the clouds, her wet face lit up in a big smile.

Sprinting out of the room, she bent down with arms extended behind her, and gave McDuff a kiss on the top of his head. "Do you want to take him for a walk?" I asked, handing her the red leash.

Eyes sparkling, her head bobbed up and down. She and McDuff walked around the busy emergency room twice, to everyone's delight. When we left that day, the doctors and nurses were beaming, as well as most of the emergency room patients who were able to smile.

Becoming the therapy dog that comforted the little girl that day was a long process. Let me tell you what it took to get him there.

Nothing should be impossible for a dog that won the trophy, first place blue ribbon, and received the highest score ever given by his instructor in obedience school. That was more than reason enough to think he would breeze through beginning agility class, rise to the top, and compete with the best of them.

McDuff had other ideas. The agility class I enrolled him in after obedience training wasn't one of them.

Everything began smoothly the first night. I stood there with a feeling of smug superiority while the small class of excited owners listened to the instructor. "Please, line up with your dogs in single file. We're going to start by having them jump over low hurdles."

This was going to be so easy. McDuff wouldn't have any problem with that, even on those short legs. On the first round, he barely cleared the bars. On the next go round, the instructor provided us with a small baton for the dogs to carry in their mouths as they jumped.

That's when McDuff balked. *Take your pick. Jump or carry the stick. I'm not doing both.* After coaxing, then threatening him to take the baton, that stubborn Scottie dug in and came down with a severe case of lockjaw. Trying to open the mouth of a Scottie with lockjaw is like trying to open a bear trap with a straw. Forget about it.

The instructor stood by watching my struggle with McDuff for several minutes. The other owners and dogs waited in line behind us becoming more impatient by the minute. "Please, step aside with your dog and let the next dog in line proceed," she instructed.

With a reassuring smile, she approached us and said, "Don't fret about it. He'll come around. All dogs love to carry and fetch things. Give him some time and work with him before you come back next week."

She didn't know my dog — I did. Carrying that baton in his mouth on command seemed too much like performing a trick to him. That was the first and last agility class for McDuff.

On my way out after class, disappointed and frustrated, I spied a flyer on the bulletin board soliciting therapy dogs. *What the heck is a therapy dog?* Taking the flyer to the instructor, I inquired about it.

"Animal assisted therapy programs use dogs to visit nursing homes, hospitals, assisted living facilities, and other places. It's well documented that dogs and other pets relieve stress. The dogs accept unconditionally, and don't judge people with disabilities, illnesses, or emotional disorders," she informed me.

"Go to the office and ask for information on Therapy Dogs International (TDI) and the American Kennel Club (AKC) Canine Good Citizen® Test."

I found out that TDI is a non-profit organization founded in 1976 by an American nurse working at a hospital in England. She observed the positive reaction of patients to daily visits of a chaplain and his dog. She returned to the States and began recruiting volunteers and dogs to visit hospitals.

TDI is the oldest registry of therapy dogs in the United States, but there are other therapy dog organizations across the country.

A dog must possess a good temperament to become a therapy dog, and completion of a basic obedience course is recommended. It cannot display aggression toward other animals and people. A health record form signed by a licensed veterinarian is mandatory.

Although it doesn't apply to other therapy dog programs like Therapy Dogs Incorporated, Therapy Dog United, and the Delta Society, TDI requires a dog and owner to pass the AKC

Canine Good Citizen Test for certification. But, the test would benefit all dog owners by making good citizens of their dogs.

My spirits lifted. This sounded like something perfect for McDuff. Maybe agility class didn't pan out for a reason. I filled out the application to sign us up, and inquired about the AKC test.

I learned a dog must be at least one year old to take the AKC Canine Good Citizen Test for therapy dog certification. The test consists of ten parts that examine a dog's temperament around people and other dogs, basic obedience, appearance, and grooming.

Reaction to distractions and supervised separation comprise a part of the testing. It presented a challenge, but I knew McDuff would meet it without difficulty.

We trained hard in the evenings after work and on weekends. As usual, McDuff picked up everything right away. The part of the test regarding distractions worried me a little. I knew people would beat on pots, pans, and other objects to create a lot of noise. Still, I had faith in my dog, and believed he'd come through it fine.

The evening arrived for the evaluator from TDI to come to obedience school and administer the test. When I entered the building, the number of participants milling around surprised me. The place teemed with excited, barking dogs and their enthusiastic owners. A long table by the wall on the back side of the room with several people manning it contained neatly stacked evaluation sheets to score each dog.

The muscular, short, crew-cut evaluator from TDI stood in front of the table and surveyed the boisterous scene. He reminded me of a Marine drill sergeant standing there taking it all in. He gave the signal, and the long evening of testing began.

A lot of dogs flunked out that cold January night. They were either too excited, scared out of their wits by the loud banging of pots and pans, or intimidated by the people using walkers or rolling around in wheelchairs.

Many refused to stay calmly with a stranger for three minutes while its owner hid out of sight. But, one part of the distraction test doomed those that did get through to the end.

The evaluator walked by all the dogs flashing a doggie treat. He waved it around in the air above his head for all the dogs to see before walking to the center of the floor and letting it drop.

Then, he instructed the owners to walk across the room with their dogs within three feet of the treat, and command the dog to ignore it while passing by. Requesting them to stroll by an Alpo® assembly line on an empty stomach would have been easier.

I watched the larger dogs drag their handlers, struggling to hold them back, over to the tempting morsel, and gobble it down. One fluffy Shih Tzu looked like a dust mop with propellers spinning around and around on its leash while its handler attempted to yank it away. Everyone howled as the lady walked away red-faced, eyes downcast.

McDuff watched it all with interest. Not many dogs had been persuaded to leave the treat alone. Finally, our turn came to take the walk. Giving him the signal to proceed, I watched his eyes zero in on the treat, mouth smacking, as we drew closer to it.

When we drew even with the goodie, he angled toward it ready to scarf it down. "No!" I said under my breath. He immediately turned away, eyes ahead, without breaking stride.

The evaluator slowly shook his head as he walked back to the evaluation table to record the final test result. "That Scottish terrier is something else," I heard him tell the woman seated at the table.

Once again, he had gone to the head of the class. My McDuff was a certified TDI therapy dog. His real work on the mission to help others could begin.

The red nylon leash I bought for McDuff's therapy dog work became the most important thing in his life. It meant a ride in the car to a place where love and attention rained down on him. That leash became an important part of his life and a symbol of his outstanding therapy dog work to me.

Wearing the red vest that I purchased later was another matter. He hated it. But, he loathed having anything put on his body.

He didn't react when I picked up the brown leather leash used in obedience class and on daily walks. It was a different story as soon as my hand touched the red leash. His ears perked up, eyes flashed, and a little dance ensued. He even grudgingly submitted to the dreaded grooming.

Therapy dogs must be clean and groomed for all therapy dog visits. That called for a bath, although I often used a dry or spray shampoo product along with a thorough brushing. McDuff hated all the grooming, but there was one part he liked — getting his teeth brushed.

Let's face it. He cared more about eating the bacon flavored toothpaste than getting his teeth to sparkle. I used peppermint breath spray in his mouth to defeat doggie breath and kept his nails clipped short. He looked spiffy for those visits, and I believe that he knew it.

Our first unsupervised therapy dog visit was to Grant Hospital to see our friend, Harvey, an artist who had spent many afternoons in Franklin Park sketching McDuff. I worried that the flow of heavy traffic and imposing high-rise buildings in downtown Columbus might intimidate McDuff. I shouldn't have, because he took it all in stride.

Something occurred to me the minute we entered the hospital lobby. We'd have to ride the elevator up to the fourth floor to see Harvey.

McDuff generated a lot of attention as we stood waiting for the elevator. It was packed after everyone got on. I had no idea how he would react to the ride and all the people crowded around him. The elevator started to rise. McDuff's head jerked. He looked up at me. *Wait a minute. What's going on here?*

"Its okay, Duff," I quickly reassured him. He firmly planted all four feet on the elevator floor and dug in. I breathed a sigh of relief. With him, I never knew when that stubborn streak would kick in and cause me grief.

Surprised, Harvey clasped his hands together in glee and laughed when he saw us. A nurse entered the room and stopped in mid-stride, startled to see a dog standing there. McDuff dashed over to her with his tail wagging like a flag in the breeze.

"Come and see what we have in here," she called out the door to the other nurses on the floor.

They came in one by one and made a big fuss over him. He loved all the attention. After they returned to their duties, he ambled over to the door periodically. With head protruding into the hallway, he watched to see if anyone else was coming to see him.

McDuff's cough drop stealing talent enabled him to amaze patients, their family members, and hospital staff in his therapy dog work. He demonstrated it in rehab/physical therapy using Halloween candy from a jar on the receptionist's desk.

Another volunteer and I entered with our dogs for a visit. The receptionist was offering treats to patients and family members who accompanied them.

"Can the dogs have a piece of candy?" she asked.

We gave our consent. She removed a piece of hard candy, pealed off the paper, and gave it to the golden retriever. She removed another piece to give to McDuff.

"You don't have to remove the wrapper, and he likes the red suckers," I said as she reached into the candy jar.

She stared at me for a moment and replied, "I don't want him to get sick from eating the paper."

"It'll be alright. Give it to him and watch what he does," I assured her.

She found a red sucker and offered it to McDuff. He gently took it from her hand and moved the top part around in his mouth using his sharp teeth and his tongue to tear holes in the covering.

Dropping the sticky treat on the floor, he spat out the paper. Then, picking up the candy, he chewed it, and let the stick fall out of his mouth.

I heard the lady say to her colleagues after she dashed out of the room, "You won't believe this. Come and watch what McDuff does when I give him a sucker."

The staff and everyone in rehab gathered around and watched him perform the feat again. Afterwards, I remarked, "He can shell a peanut, remove the skin, and eat it, too."

On our next therapy dog visit, peanuts in the shell awaited him. His demonstrations lightened tension, and put a smile on everyone's face. McDuff made days brighter and the rehabilitation process easier for many people.

Doctors, nurses, and other professionals at the hospitals enjoyed therapy dog visits as much as the patients. Nursing stations on each floor kept dog biscuits in the desk drawers for them. McDuff was short and a little pudgy to begin with and started to pork up from eating so many. I substituted diet biscuits for the nurses to give him as his treat. He never knew the difference. That's one of the few times I was able to fool him.

During the time that we visited hospital floors, rehabilitation centers, and emergency rooms, McDuff's effect on people never failed to amaze me. Everyone, including the professional staff, perked up at the sight of him. The same magic occurred in nursing homes and assisted living facilities.

Elderly occupants cried while reminiscing about the dogs they were forced to leave behind, or had owned during their lifetime. Many, alone in the world, had no one to visit or care about them. Whenever McDuff entered the room, smiles and laughter cut through their loneliness. Being able to hug something that gave back warm kisses, affection, and unconditional love lifted their spirits and warmed their hearts. I observed first hand how he reached out to a withdrawn, elderly man one afternoon.

I was glad only one room remained at the conclusion of our therapy dog visit at the hospital. Unlike the volunteer with her large golden retriever, I had to lift a chunky Scottie onto each bed. Feeling weary, I neared the room at the end of the hall and was stopped by a nurse.

"The old man in there refuses to respond to anyone. Maybe you'll want to pass on that room," she said in a whisper.

With a sense of relief, I turned to walk away. McDuff had something else in mind. He pulled me into the room and stood waiting for the happy reception he'd been receiving everywhere.

The bed was rumpled and empty, but a high-back chair in the corner held a frail, white-haired man. His body, almost invisible under the white blanket wrapped around him, slumped over. His chin pressed down on his chest.

*Is he asleep? Maybe I shouldn't wake him*, I thought.

"Hello. Do you want a visit from a therapy dog?" I asked.

No answer. Before I could decide whether to stay or leave, McDuff dragged me across the room, stood in front of him, tail wagging like crazy. The man didn't move his slight frame, but lifted his eyes and stared at McDuff. That was all the invitation McDuff needed to rest his head on the man's knee and return the gaze.

"McDuff's a therapy dog, and he visits patients here in hospital," I said, thinking it might elicit a response.

The man ignored me and directed his attention to McDuff. Slowly, he raised his withered hand and placed it on McDuff's head.

I waited for him to say something or recognize my presence. The room remained silent.

"Have a good day," I said after waiting for a while.

We turned and walked away. When we reached the doorway, I heard a feeble voice say softly, "Thank you."

The nurse and I made the decision that the lonely man didn't want a visit, but therapy dog McDuff knew better.

# CHAPTER 5

# The Bright Light

*Forgiveness is the fragrance that*
*the violet sheds on the heel that*
*has crushed it.*

—MARK TWAIN

THE DEATH OF A CLOSE FAMILY MEMBER, MARITAL SEPARATION, AND divorce are on the list of the five most stressful events in a person's life. I experienced them all within one year. McDuff's presence comforted and helped me withstand the stress and strain.

He was sent to guide me through those dark days and, at the same time, teach me valuable lessons that changed me forever.

My second marriage had been shaky for quite some time. Loss of trust is a death blow to any relationship. Perhaps, I had a premonition, because I didn't change my last name when I remarried. The decision to end the union was inevitable, but it carried a price I found hard to pay.

It meant losing McDuff. How I hated to face that. After all, he wasn't mine, but a Christmas present from me to my husband. He loved him as much as I did. I knew he would want to take him away from me.

The thought of giving up McDuff broke my heart. However, the horrendous event preceding my husband's moving out made ending the marriage unavoidable.

My husband and I agreed that he would look for an apartment so he could move out. Tension sparked like lightning bolts across a stormy sky as we shared the mutual living space. One evening, I reclined in a living room chair with my legs comfortably stretched out across the ottoman. He sat on the sofa nearby eating dinner from a solid wood snack tray while watching television.

Bickering between us began. It escalated and all the pent-up anger and resentment in him came bubbling to the surface. Without warning, he exploded.

Relaxed, caught completely off guard, I watched him spring up, lift the tray and swing it at me, aiming for my head. He picked it up and brought it hurtling down with such force and velocity that the dinner plate flew through the air. The plate shattered, hit, and cut my left wrist as I raised my arms to protect my head and face. It all happened so fast.

Poor McDuff tore out of the room and headed for the safety of the recreation room on the lower level. The frightening crash of the tray, coupled with the violent atmosphere between the two people he loved, terrified him, causing him to flee.

Despite the shock of seeing blood dripping down my hand to the floor, and concern for him, my attention riveted on something else.

After the blow from the tray, I waited for pain to wash over me, or some ill effect from what had to be life-threatening injuries. That's when I became aware of it — the brightest, most magnificent light imaginable.

Looking through it, my husband's face, contorted in rage, his eyes bulging, veins jutting out on the sides of his neck, was visible on the other side. Without hesitating, he raised the tray again and brought it crashing down full force on my extended legs on the foot stool.

But, all I thought of the whole time this went on was, *what is that bright light?* My mind blocked out everything else. Then, the dazzling light faded and disappeared.

My husband towered over me, probably wondering why my head hadn't fallen off. I wondered the same thing as I sat there too stunned to move, and afraid to try getting up on what surely must be two broken legs. *Why no pain? Why am I still alive?* I wondered in disbelief. I felt no pain anywhere in my body.

He stepped back watching me for I don't know what. I gathered enough courage to attempt to stand. To my surprise, I rose to my feet without any problem and stood in front of him. We stared at each other.

The room was strangely silent; the only sound his heavy breathing. But, he wasn't finished with me yet. No way did he intend to let me out of that room alive.

Facing him, with an eerie sense of tranquility enveloping me, I watched him ball up his hands and advance menacingly toward me, seething rage twisting his features with every step closer. When he got near enough to hit me, the oddest thing happened.

With raised fist, he spun around in a circle and ended up about five feet away from me. He paused for a moment. Then, he sprang at me again poised to strike once more — the same thing happened. I watched him twirl away.

Puzzled, I thought, *what's the matter with him?* His labored breathing cut through the stillness as he stood there, both arms hanging innocently by his sides. "Why don't you hit me," I said in a voice dripping in scorn. He turned, stormed out of the room, and down the steps to the lower level where McDuff cowered.

It all took place in a matter of minutes, but it seemed like an eternity. Walking over to the telephone, I dialed 911.

"My husband attacked me, and I want the police to come," I told the voice on the line.

"Are you hurt?"

"Yes, my wrist is bleeding, but the flow has almost stopped. My legs are badly bruised."

"Where is your husband? Is he near you now?"

"No, he's downstairs."

"Don't worry. The police are on the way. I'll stay on the line with you until they arrive."

Two squad cars arrived within minutes. One of the officers removed my husband from the premises, and the other offered to take me to the hospital, but I declined. The cut had stopped bleeding, and despite bruises, miraculously, my legs weren't injured.

I filed a report with the officer. My husband was handcuffed and taken away in one of the squad cars. After the officer left, I remembered McDuff.

I ran down the steps to check on him and found him huddled in a corner trembling. Calling him to me, I held him, talking softly while I tried to soothe him. Doing that calmed me down, too. But, not for long. Red hot waves of revenge consumed me as I sat on the floor holding McDuff.

Kelly was livid when I called and told him of the attack the next day. He lived in his own apartment nearby and rushed over to check on me.

"Do you want me to stay with you when he gets out of jail, Mom?" he said in a voice full of concern.

"No. I'll be alright."

I seethed with hatred and thoughts of revenge every time the attack came to mind. Filled with resentment and thinking only of retaliation, I forgot about the strange light.

Shortly after, I visited my mother in Springfield. Just before I left to drive back to Columbus, she hugged me good-bye and said, "You know, every night I pray for God to put his angels around you and your house."

My mother didn't know the full story about our breakup. Telling her about the physical assault would have devastated and upset her. I didn't want her to worry about me. What she said resonated in my mind on the drive back home.

But, I hadn't seen any celestial beings with wings, only an incredibly bright light. It nagged at me until I went to the library and checked out a book on angels. I read that angels can manifest as bright lights, and were referred to as beings of light.

I believe my guardian angel protected me from harm on that fateful day. It appeared as the intense, translucent light between us while my husband struck me with the tray. It prevented him from striking me with his fists by spinning him away from me and across the room. There is no doubt in my mind that is the reason I am alive today.

The dreaded day came when my husband and a friend, escorted by a police officer, came to gather his personal belongings — and McDuff. The restraining order I obtained after he was released from jail prevented him from coming to collect his things without first making arrangements.

To hide my despair, I tried to put up a brave front when they walked in the door. Bad enough to deal with acid feelings of failure and bitterness about the marriage, but losing McDuff on top of that made it unbearable.

After packing his things, he turned to his friend and said, "I'm taking my dog, too." Evidently, that was the first time his friend heard about it.

"Look, I told you that you could stay with me for a while, but you didn't say anything about a dog. That's out. No, the dog can't come," he said wagging his finger at McDuff.

My husband argued passionately to change his frowning companion's mind. Sensing an opportunity, I spoke up. "If you leave without him, that's it. You can't come back and get him later." Reluctantly, he agreed to leave McDuff and relinquish any future claims to him.

I didn't betray my emotions outwardly, but inside, my heart jumped for joy. McDuff sat there taking it all in. He didn't care about all the commotion concerning him. All he saw was conflict between two people he loved, not the domestic violence and discord.

I became a "victim of domestic violence" in the legal system after the attack. That term is all wrong. Yes, there is violence involved, but the "victim" is not the individual assaulted. It's the one who loses control and harms another. And, the perpetrator should have to suffer the consequences of that despicable act.

However, my husband hadn't been violent toward me before the incident that day. On the contrary, he treated me well during our marriage. I didn't have much contact with him after it happened, but I remember he apologized and told me, "I just snapped."

All I know is that something wonderful came out of that bad experience, the bright light. I will feel its peace and protection forever.

I wish my ex-husband well, and harbor no hard feelings toward him now. It took me years to get to that point, though. The turbulent waves of divorce don't have to leave discord and hatred in their wake. My first husband, Mel, and I are the best of friends — more like family than friends.

We graduated from high school together and married shortly after. Our families knew each other before we were born. My parents considered him the son they never had. It remained that way until the day they died, even though we were no longer married. Juanita, Mel's present wife, is as beautiful inside as she is outside. I'm glad he found someone special like her to share his life.

My belief is that good comes out of every situation, even the ones that appear negative at the time. The good thing is that the end of my marriage forced me to take a hard look and examine myself. Coming face to face with my critical, judgmental side, prompted me to make changes.

The time I spent learning to forgive and make peace with myself made me a much better person in the end. I know there is good in everything that happens to us — even the seemingly bad things — if we choose to learn from them and evolve.

How many people let life pass them by while obsessing about an ex-spouse who's probably not giving them a second thought? I made the decision to move on to freedom, happiness, and a new life.

Perhaps, I experienced relief at the end of the marriage, but McDuff was miserable after his master left. He hung on the back of the sofa anxiously watching out of the living room window for hours, day after day, all the while giving me soulful looks. *Where is he? When is he coming home?*

McDuff didn't judge; he didn't condemn; he chose to see only the good in his master. My heart ached for him, but there was nothing I could do to end his misery. At the time, my husband may have been the scum of the earth to me, but our problems didn't matter to McDuff.

It seems easier for dogs to love unconditionally and forgive than humans. Is it because we find it hard to understand that type of love, loyalty, and devotion? After a while, McDuff spent less time at his watchtower and accepted it would be the two of us.

We had adjustments to make, and we helped each other through them. And then, just when my life returned to normal, my world came crashing down. My time with McDuff was sharply curtailed during the coming months, but the quality of time, and not the quantity of time, mattered most.

CHAPTER 6

# Home Invasion

*Whatever comes, this too*
*shall pass away.*
—ELLA WHEELER WILCOX

THE EVENING OF FEBRUARY 1, 1999 SIGNALED THE BEGINNING OF A heartbreaking and emotional rollercoaster ride. My mother lived in the red brick house that once belonged to my grandmother. After my grandmother's death, Mom and Dad moved from Uniontown, Pennsylvania to Springfield, Ohio. The move brought them closer to me since Columbus was only fifty miles away.

After Dad died, Mom lived in the huge house alone. She and the other widows living on Center Street checked on and looked out for each other daily. Blanche lived directly across the street from Mom. Another friend, Minnie, lived nearby. They were like family to me.

We exchanged Christmas and birthday gifts. Each year I gave them all Easter baskets and the biggest Easter lilies I could find. I detected something terribly wrong the moment I heard Blanche's trembling voice.

"Judy, a man broke into your mom's house a little while ago. She escaped and ran across the street to my place," Blanche spoke, her words all tumbling together. "She wasn't harmed, but she's having trouble breathing. I called the emergency squad, and they're on the way."

McDuff sensed my anxiety as I stood stunned after hanging up the phone. He never took his eyes off my face, and stayed on my heels as I scurried around preparing to leave. I took time to gather up dog food for him and that was it. To be truthful, I wasn't thinking clearly enough to organize anything else.

Putting on my warmest coat and hat, I raced down the steps to the garage with McDuff running behind me. I knew the hospital where Mom would be taken. With an unsteady hand, I turned the key in the ignition and headed out into the darkness with trepidation.

It normally took an hour to get to Springfield from Columbus, but that night I got there in thirty minutes. I drove my navy blue Honda ninety-five miles per hour passing everything on the road.

I thought if a highway patrolman stopped me, I'd get escorted to the hospital. That didn't happen. I'm lucky I wasn't thrown in jail for speeding. As I said earlier, clear thinking didn't prevail that evening.

Roaring into the hospital parking lot, I circled around until I found an open space. "McDuff, stay," I said, preventing him from following me out of the car. I knew he'd be all right. He never barked or fussed when left in the car, and his black coat made him invisible in the dark. I raced into the emergency room and ran up to the lady at the receiving desk.

"I'm Virginia Jones' daughter from Columbus. Her neighbor called and said the squad brought her here," I said, panting while trying to regain my breath.

She motioned for someone who led me to a cubicle encircled by long white curtains. My heart sank when I looked inside. Mom lay on the bed with her eyes closed, surrounded by doctors and nurses working frantically to revive her. Tubes came out of every opening in her body, and a dark fluid drained into a bag on the side of the bed. An oxygen mask obscured her small face. *Am I too late?*

I watched helplessly. The medical team, so intent on their tasks, didn't notice me standing there at first. Mom moaned and moved her head. I realized she was still alive, although semiconscious. One of the doctors glanced up, took my arm, and led me aside.

"You're her daughter?" He didn't wait for an answer. "She's in critical condition. I don't expect her to pull through." He showed me an X-ray on the wall and pointed to the sinister fluid drowning her lungs. "She has pneumonia on top of congestive heart failure."

I remembered Blanche telling me earlier how Mom ran out of her house into the cold night. It was a source of amusement for me the way she always wore a coat or sweater even in the warmest weather. I always teased her about it. It broke my heart to think of her running for her life into the cold winter's eve without the cane she used to help her walk.

After stabilization, they moved her from the emergency room to the Intensive Care Unit. I called Minnie and told her I was on the way to drop McDuff off. Entering the car, I found him patiently waiting for me. I hugged him for a minute. Burying my face in his thick fur relaxed me.

"We're going to see Minnie, Duff," I said starting the engine.

She stood at the door waiting for us. News travels fast in a small town. Blanche had called her. McDuff loved visiting, because she had a large, fenced-in back yard, and she spoiled him rotten. She called him her "little angel."

Living alone after her husband died and being childless, she was more than happy to look after McDuff. She offered a place for me to stay when I wasn't at the hospital.

After dropping McDuff off, I rushed back to the hospital and spent most of the next four weeks in ICU. Those who have been subjected to having a family member hospitalized in critical condition know the trauma and emotional turmoil involved.

Fortunately, the hospital had a lenient policy regarding ICU and family member visitors. I appreciated having permission to stay with my mother and sleep in her room during her stay there. The nurses provided a reclining chair, pillow, and blanket for me. But, there's not much sleeping with nurses and doctors shuffling in and out at all hours of the night.

Days of brushing my teeth and taking birdbaths in the ladies restroom sink faced me, along with hospital cafeteria meals when my stomach permitted it. I became friends with the other lost souls I encountered in the waiting room and cafeteria.

"How's your mom today? Any improvement?" They'd ask.

"Not yet. What about your dad? Was the surgery successful?"

We tried to support and encourage each other.

Mom, listed in critical condition and heavily sedated, looked so small and vulnerable lying in the hospital bed hooked up to everything imaginable. Less than five feet tall, she barely weighed over ninety pounds. Tears trickled down my cheeks as I stroked her soft white hair.

The vital signs monitor beside the bed beeped with each beat of her heart, numbers flashed measuring heart rhythm and rate, oxygen level, respiration, and blood pressure. My eyes became hypnotized by the changing numbers. I don't know why, because I wasn't knowledgeable enough to understand what they meant.

The smell of rubbing alcohol mixed with disinfectant tingled in my nose. Intravenous bags of nourishment and medication swung from hooks on a pole-like stand beside her bed. Neighbors started to arrive, distressed about what had happened to Mom, and offering their support.

Blanche relayed what my mother said about the break-in before the ambulance arrived. Mom told her that she had been sitting in her living room watching television around ten p.m. and heard the sound of glass shattering at the back of the house on the enclosed porch.

Going to her dining room, she gazed into the kitchen where she had a view of the locked kitchen door. It disintegrated and a man burst through. Their eyes locked. She ran into the night screaming at the top of her lungs.

Blanche called on the man who lived next door to her for help. He sprinted across the street and found Mom's front door wide open. Rushing in to investigate, he saw a man he recognized standing in the middle of the living room taking something from my mother's purse.

When confronted, the man dropped the purse, bolted past him, and fled down the street. The police arrived within minutes and scoured the neighborhood. Several days later, the man turned himself in.

It helped me to know the details of what happened to my mother. But, whether she'd survive the ordeal became my uppermost concern at the moment. An overpowering need to get away from the hospital for a while engulfed me. The grind of hearing about everything, and the atmosphere of the ICU, overwhelmed me. I had to escape.

Escaping to Minnie's house gave me a respite from the hospital and an opportunity to take a shower and try to get some sleep. McDuff danced and twirled in delight to see me. The nights I stayed there, he slept in the bed close to me, his back resting against my legs as I fell into an exhausted slumber. And, he was there for Minnie, too.

Once, upon awakening early from an uneasy sleep, I heard her talking to him in the kitchen. "Angel, what do you want for breakfast this morning? Sausage or bacon with your eggs?" He ate what she ate for breakfast.

In the evenings, when Minnie sat in her chair watching television, McDuff jumped up on her lap. They fell asleep together. He recognized her loneliness and stayed close to comfort her. I know, because McDuff wasn't a lap dog.

While I stayed at the hospital with Mom, he rendered therapy dog treatment to Minnie. And on the few nights I slept there, he administered to me, too. After spending a night in my oasis with them, I returned to the desert atmosphere of the ICU.

To the doctors' amazement, Mom continued to hold on. After the first week in ICU, one of her doctors took me aside after examining her. "Mrs. McFadden, it's just a matter of time. She won't live much longer in her condition."

The funny thing is she told me all about that conversation when she was well enough to talk. She overheard and understood every word. We laughed about it. Mom continued to hang on day after day with slight improvement.

The doctors expected her to die at any time. They saw a frail, old lady suffering from heart failure and serious multiple complications. To them, she didn't stand a chance, but they didn't know the tenacious woman who hit every curve ball that life threw at her out of the ballpark.

Seventy-nine years old, diagnosed with heart failure, pneumonia, and an infection that caused a raging fever, Mom had an uphill battle to recovery. On top of that, another medical problem existed. The doctor in the emergency room asked me about insulin shots at the time she was admitted.

When I told him she wasn't diabetic, he explained the onset of diabetes resulted from the fight or flight reflex. It caused blood glucose levels to rise rapidly over a short period of time. After I learned more about the reflex, I understood what my poor mother went through during her flight on that frigid, winter night.

Alone in a house at night startled by the sound of shattering glass, she jerked. Heart pounding. Blood pressure shooting up. Beads of perspiration turned into a full-blown sweat to cool her body. Eyes wide in fright, pupils dilated for better vision. Every muscle tense. Breath escaping in short pants.

She tipped-toed out of the living room and peered through the dining room into the kitchen. Glucose and hormone levels shot up at alarming rates. Any bodily function not related to defense or escape suppressed or decreased.

The fight or flight reflex transformed Mom into Wonder Woman on the spot — supercharged with greater strength, faster speed, pain resistant. Violently, the door broke apart from repeated powerful kicks. A sinister shadow jumped out of the darkness. A man advanced toward her.

In that terrifying instant, she made the crucial decision — she chose flight over fight and fled to safety.

One afternoon in the hospital when she was able to speak, Mom told me the name of the man who broke into her home. She described how she ran out into the cold in her slippers, without hat or coat, wearing a thin housecoat. The cane she needed to get around left forgotten on the living room floor.

She told me she didn't stop screaming until she ran all the way across the street and pounded on Blanche's front door. I rocked her frail body in my arms as she talked. She never mentioned it again.

Another week passed and one by one the tubes and oxygen mask went away. She sat up in bed for brief periods, digested liquid foods, and grew a little stronger each day. My confidence soared, believing good days and recovery lay ahead. I didn't know then that something would soon destroy that positive outlook.

# CHAPTER 7

# Through the Storm

*I answered the heroic question,*
*"Death, where is thy sting?" with,*
*"It is here in my heart and mind and memories."*
— MAYA ANGELOU

MIRACULOUSLY, AFTER TWO WEEKS IN ICU, ALTHOUGH SEDATED AND disoriented at times, Mom survived through the worst of it. Her improved condition gave me an opportunity to get away from the hospital and return to Columbus for a few days. I longed for a good night's sleep in my own bed and the comforts of my own home.

Minnie felt glad for Mom's recovery, but sad about her "little angel" going home. We had tears in our eyes as we hugged good-bye. I left and got home around six p.m. after stopping at Wendy's for a burger and fries, and the neighborhood carryout to pick up a newspaper.

McDuff stretched out on the floor by my chair, satisfied after sharing a portion of my hamburger. The brass, queen-size bed upstairs beckoned to me. I couldn't wait to stretch out on it for a good night's sleep.

The telephone rang at seven p.m. intruding on my vision of slumber. *Who could that be? No one knows I'm back yet.* The ICU night nurse's strained voice came over the line and jerked me to attention.

"Judy, I don't know how to tell you this," she said in a voice choked with emotion.

"What's wrong?" *Please don't tell me my mother died,* I thought, tasting fear in my mouth.

"Your mother fell out of her bed headfirst onto the floor. She's in X-ray now. It doesn't look good."

It's impossible to describe what went through my mind, and I don't recall what I said over the phone. What I do remember is falling to the floor after I hung up the phone, screaming, "God, please, lighten up," through sobs. McDuff pressed up against my body, licking my face, sensing my anguish. I clung to him and croaked, "We have to go back, Duff."

I didn't drive at breakneck speed this time. In a daze and unaware of the highway and scenery flashing by, my hands gripped the steering wheel like two claws. My composure slipped away, and I spiraled downward into despair. Empty and too drained to cry, all I could think to do was pray.

McDuff sat quietly watching me as the words sputtered out of my mouth. Before long, I felt a warm blanket of calmness wrap around me. By the time I reached the hospital, control reigned once more.

The nurses rushed up to me as I stepped out of the elevator. "Judy, I'm so sorry. We don't know how it could have happened," one of them said, her face stained from tears.

I tried my best to concentrate on their words through the mist in my mind. Because of Mom's continuous high fever, the regular hospital mattress had been replaced with a cooling mattress. Can you imagine lying on a sheet of solid ice? Because of the cooling device inside, it made the height of her bed from the hard, uncarpeted floor higher than usual.

My mind's eye conjured up a terrible image — Mom, her head covered by a large bandage, suffering from brain damage, and a fractured skull. I slumped against the hallway wall awaiting her return from X-ray.

The elevator door opened and the clacking of rolling wheels reverberated down the long hallway. *This is it. Prepare yourself.* As the two white-coated orderlies pushed the bed closer, I searched it to see the tiny woman I so dearly loved. I couldn't believe the sight before my eyes.

A broad smile beamed from my mother's face and her eyes twinkled as she met my astonished gaze. There wasn't a bandage, fractured skull, or brain damage, just an egg-sized lump on her forehead. I stood nailed to the spot with the nurses standing just as dumbfounded beside me. Then, they scrambled to get her settled back in her room.

"Mom, what happened? How did you fall out of your bed?" I asked after the still shaken nurses left.

"I tried to pick up a piece of paper that fell on the floor. I leaned over and that's the last thing I remember."

"Your guardian angel watched over you. A bright light saved me once, too," I replied squeezing her warm, moist hand. Sinking into an exhausted sleep, she didn't hear a word I'd said.

People asked me why I didn't sue the hospital for negligence. The thought never entered my mind. I'd been in my mother's room day and night for weeks, and witnessed the hard work and dedication of her nurses. What occurred devastated them. I couldn't find it in my heart to fault them.

Mom showed no ill effects from her swan dive. She regained her strength with each passing day. After another week in ICU, she was transferred out to a regular room. I celebrated with the staff on the floor, and with mixed emotions, we said our good-byes.

Every chance I got I stopped by to chat with the nurses and report on Mom's progress. We speculated about her going home someday. But, someday wasn't soon enough for Mom.

She recuperated enough to become impatient, irritable, and tired of being in the hospital. Who could blame her? She wanted to get out and go home to finish convalescence. And, she wouldn't take "no" for an answer. Everyone made her angry by denying her repeated requests to go home.

The doctors and I bore the brunt of her wrath. She reasoned being out of ICU meant she was well enough to receive care at home. Of course, that wasn't the case. Because of the severity of her medical condition, she still had a long way to go.

Trying to soothe and reason with her only made her angrier, more frustrated, and uncooperative. It became a struggle to get her to do anything. She stopped eating. In went the feeding tube, again.

More and more, she sat silently staring at her hands. I could see the fight ebbing out of them. She refused to communicate with anyone, even me. The inner strength so prevalent during the previous hard weeks evaporated like dew in the morning sun. My mother gave up.

Before long, she was back in ICU — this time hooked up to life support. Hope didn't abide with me this time. The continuous beep of the monitoring equipment and regular rhythm of the respirator in the room vibrated in the space we occupied.

Oblivious to everything happening around me, I sat by her bedside as her vital organs shut down like collapsing dominoes until only one apparatus kept life in her body — the respirator.

"Judy, at her age, and in her weakened condition, she won't recover. You'll have to decide whether you want to keep her on the respirator or disconnect life support," the doctor told me.

Asking one person to make a decision when or whether another person lives or dies is a lot to ask. Many people have faced that terrible burden and made the difficult choice. I thought about the painful, intense suffering my mother endured over the previous four weeks. Her spirit and determination to fight the battle as long and hard as she did won my admiration. It was time for her to rest.

I leaned over and kissed the forehead of what remained of my mother. "Good-bye, Mom. I love you. God bless your soul," I whispered as silent tears fell.

After making the hardest decision of my life, I walked over to the nurse's station. "Call the doctor, and tell him I want to have my mother disconnected from life support."

Returning to her bedside, I waited for the doctor to be contacted, glad for the extra time with her. *Am I doing the right thing? Maybe she can still pull through.* Doubt assaulted me as I stood looking down on her peaceful face.

But, I knew even if she continued to live, she would not have good quality of life. If by some miracle she happened to survive after being taken off the respirator, then it would be between Mom and God.

It wasn't long before the nurses entered the room and began disconnecting her from the various pieces of equipment. One by one, the beeps and squeaks stopped. Only the hissing of the respirator remained until it ceased to move. All sounds disappeared — except for the nonstop beep from the flat line on the heart monitor.

Nurses gathered around me, their mouths moving, but I didn't hear any words coming out. They consoled me on the death of my mother, but they didn't know that a part of me had died, too.

My mother was pronounced dead at 5:42 p.m. I walked out of her room like a zombie to the nurse's station. Dialing the coroner first, then the police department, I reported her death as instructed when she was initially hospitalized. One sensation slipped through the mantle of emptiness that covered me, the overpowering sense of loneliness.

It hit me full force. The only child of my mother, an only child herself, and me with one son, I realized that I didn't have a big support system. My parents and grandparents were gone. Kelly lived in another state, and without sisters or brothers, and nieces or nephews, no one was around to offer comfort and support.

An overwhelming sense of loss and desolation descended upon me. I left the hospital in deep despair, but I didn't know that an epiphany awaited me at Minnie's house.

Walking through the door, I watched McDuff sprint toward me on those stubby legs, tail wagging. Then, I remembered. I hadn't been alone on those sad drives in the dark to the hospital. I hadn't been abandoned those nights he slept beside me when I was exhausted and stressed beyond belief. I hadn't been by myself when I received the terrifying telephone call to come back to the hospital when Mom fell out of her bed.

McDuff accompanied me on every one of those sad rides. He licked away the tears when I lay crying on the floor, beaten down by life. God blessed me with this extraordinary creature to walk by my side through the stormy times. No, I wasn't alone. McDuff comforted, guided, and taught me. No matter what I had to face in the future, he'd be there with me to ease the pain and provide his brand of therapy dog consolation.

# CHAPTER 8

# Trial by Jury

*We ought always to deal justly,*
*not only with those who are just to us, but likewise*
*to those who endeavor to injure us; and this, for*
*fear lest by rendering them evil for evil, we should*
*fall into the same vice.*

—HIEROCLES

A YEAR PASSED AFTER MOM'S FUNERAL BEFORE I RECEIVED A LETTER from the Clark County Prosecuting Attorney's Office advising me of the May 8, 2000 trial date. It informed me the court had granted motions to consolidate the burglary and manslaughter charges, and obtain expert witnesses on behalf of the defendant.

The prosecuting attorney would argue at trial that the home invasion and burglary proved traumatic enough to cause my mother's death weeks later. Usually, physical assault is involved in a charge of involuntary manslaughter. Conviction would set a precedent and be the first of its kind in Clark County.

My mother died twenty-seven days after the break-in and had a pre-existing heart condition. The State would have to prove cause, not intent, in her death. The trial generated tremendous attention across the nation, especially in communities and states with large senior populations.

Friends, fearing the newspaper articles they read referred to my mother, called from New York and Florida. The upcoming trial received front page coverage in the Springfield newspaper. Permission had been granted for a camera in the courtroom to record the proceedings. I didn't want the notoriety, but it wasn't about me.

Older people nationwide would benefit from a guilty verdict on the involuntary manslaughter charge where no bodily harm occurred. What happened to my mother could serve as a warning to those trusting souls, alone and vulnerable.

The man who broke into Mom's home often ate at her table. She'd hired him to work in her yard, unaware of his four prior felony convictions, including offenses of violence. A lawn service came and cut the grass, but she saved money on her fixed income by paying him to weed her flower beds.

My mother always urged people to join her for meals if they were around while she cooked. Her grandmother raised her that way. The neighbors told me the defendant often enjoyed her hospitality. Her upbringing may have contributed to her demise.

The day of the trial finally arrived. Spring is beautiful in Ohio, new and fresh, full of green leaves and flowers bursting with colorful blooms. Crops in farmer's fields beside the highway shot up through fertile soil. Ordinarily, I enjoyed the scenic drive to Springfield in May. Not this time — I dreaded every mile.

McDuff balanced on the passenger seat looking out of the window enjoying the ride. Half way there, my nerves reached the breaking point. I asked God for strength and courage to face the trial ahead. And, I don't know why, I asked for a sign about the outcome.

After driving in silence for a while, I glanced out of the side window. What I saw caused my mouth to drop open — a magnificent rainbow curved across the rain-free blue sky.

"Look at the beautiful rainbow, Duff!" I said, tingling with exhilaration.

Rainbows are special to me. As a little girl in Pennsylvania, I truly believed a pot of gold awaited me at the end. The sight of a rainbow after a thunderstorm sent me running like an

Olympic sprinter to find the treasure. I never found it, but that didn't keep me from trying every time I saw one.

The same childish surge of excitement washed over me as I looked at the arch of radiant colors that day. I cried tears of relief, accepting it as a sign that justice would prevail. Some good purpose would come out of Mom's long, painful suffering and death.

After dropping McDuff off at Minnie's, I walked into a packed courtroom. The presence of the television camera contributed to the aura of electricity that sparked in the air. The defendant and his attorney entered the room and took their places at the defense table. Court convened, and after opening statements, the State called me as its first witness. The prosecutor alerted me before court that I'd be asked to identify a photograph of my mother.

I walked to the witness stand, and sat down after being sworn in. The camera pointed my way. Aware of the eyes of the jury and courtroom observers riveted on me, I swallowed hard. A tightening in my stomach caused a shortness of breath as I gazed at the large, glossy picture thrust into my hands.

What the prosecutor failed to inform me before court was the method of identification — my mother's autopsy photograph. Giving me a moment to regain my composure, he began questioning me. I forced myself to look over at the defendant. He watched me intently as he sat beside his attorney. As our eyes locked, I couldn't believe what I saw.

*Did he just wink at me? No, that couldn't be. He must have a tic that causes him to blink one eye.* I stared at him during my testimony waiting for the tic to reoccur. It never did. He continued watching me with a slight smile on his lips.

I informed the prosecutor about it after court. He said he would speak to the defendant's attorney to ensure it never happened again. Other witnesses testified for the State, and then, the first and most difficult day ended. I didn't know how many more of them I could endure.

After the final witness testified on the second day, the State rested. The defense attorney began his case. He focused on my mother's pre-existing congestive heart failure, the long period between the break-in and her death, and the detrimental effect of the fight or flight reflex on her body. Five doctors and a retired coroner were called as expert witnesses.

Because of her month-long stay in the hospital, mainly in ICU, thousands of medical documents accrued. Stacks covered the entire floor of the prosecuting attorney's office. I saw the pure hell my mother went through while they accumulated.

I listened to the first expert doctor testify that Mom was "one sick old lady who wouldn't have lived much longer, anyway." I sat through days of excruciating, detailed accounts of four other experts about the various aspects of her failing health. The coroner described the autopsy procedure step by step, spoke of black holes in her heart, the deteriorating state of her lungs, and other vital organs.

Nothing personal to them, just another day on the job. Hearing my mother dissected and discussed sounded anything but impersonal to me. I ached to escape from that courtroom. After what seemed liked ages, the judge recessed court for fifteen minutes.

I rushed out of the courtroom and collapsed on one of the benches outside. Shortly after, the defendant's attorney popped out the door and quickly lit a cigarette. At least, he had nicotine to help him relieve his tension. I guess the pressure of the trial got to him, too.

He took a long drag, inhaled deeply on the cigarette, turned and saw me sitting there watching him. Our eyes met. Surprise registered on his face. We nodded stiffly. He hesitated a minute, then walked over to me.

"The prosecutor told me what happened in the courtroom when you were on the witness stand the other day. I want to apologize to you, and let you know I don't always have a choice of who I am called to represent. It should never have happened, and I'm truly sorry."

"It's alright. You're only doing your job. I'll be glad when all of this is over."

We walked back to the courtroom. Me, to face more agonizing testimony, and him, to continuing picking through my mother's body like a vulture.

On the third day, after closing arguments, the jury retired to deliberate. I went to the Victim Witness Division office to wait with the caring supportive people I had come to rely on. I can't say enough about Joy and the wonderful staff employed there. They did everything possible to make a grueling situation easier.

The detectives and police officers assigned to the case came by to sit with me and wait for the verdict. Mom's case clearly touched them. I think, because she could have been anybody's mother who lived alone — helpless and victimized.

When a verdict didn't come at the end of the day, I went to Minnie's house to spend the night as I'd done throughout the proceedings.

McDuff met me at the door as usual. He provided therapy to Minnie and me throughout the trial, and he didn't let either one of us down. Holding and petting him calmed me after long, stressful days in court more than the nicotine in the defense attorney's cigarettes. Having him there helped me keep my sanity. He had hung with me through the worst times of my life.

On May 11, the jury concluded deliberations. I returned to the courtroom, my stomach tied up in a knot. I knew a lot was at stake. A guilty verdict would put predators on notice, and send a loud and clear message.

To enter the jury box, the jury had to file past the first row where I stood. Seven men and five women walked by me in single file, all eyes deliberately avoiding mine — except for one lanky man with a beard. His eyes burned into mine, and he held my gaze as he walked by. I had no idea what to make of it. Was it a good or a bad sign?

"Ladies and gentlemen of the jury, have you reached a verdict in this case?" the judge inquired of the foreman.

"Yes, Your Honor."

The man who looked directly at me on his way into the courtroom, rose and handed the verdict form to the bailiff.

The bailiff returned it to him after the judge read the form. I could feel my heart pounding in my chest as he prepared to read the verdict. My pulse raced, the blood pounded in my head.

"Please inform the court of your verdict," said the Judge.

I held my breath as he began to speak.

"We find the defendant . . . guilty on Count One of Burglary."

It was a given he'd be found guilty of burglary. An eye witness saw him in Mom's house with her purse in his hands after he stole twenty dollars from it. A guilty verdict on the involuntary manslaughter charge would be the precedent-setting one.

"We find the defendant . . . guilty on Count Two of Involuntary Manslaughter."

The courtroom erupted. I hugged Minnie and rushed over to the prosecutor to thank him for all his hard work and dedication. The judge set May 23 as the sentencing date, and court adjourned.

The May 12, 2000 *Columbus Dispatch* trumpeted in bold print, "Handyman found guilty of scaring woman to death." Clamoring reporters and a cameraman with blinding lights waited outside the courtroom to interview me after the trial ended. Drained and exhausted, I responded to their requests for a statement. The jury's verdict sent a message to those who preyed on elderly women living alone. My mother's death had not been in vain.

The day of sentencing arrived. I found myself at the Clark County Courthouse again, but this time with the burden of the trial lifted from my shoulders. I could go on with my life in peace. Sleep eluded me the previous night as my mind raced thinking about how I wanted to address the court.

Court convened. After opening formalities, the judge turned to me.

"The victim's daughter wishes to make a statement before sentencing. Mrs. McFadden, would you please stand?"

Despite all the eyes in the courtroom focused on me, I wasn't nervous when I rose from my seat and started to speak.

"One of the defense expert doctors testified that my mother was 'one sick old lady who didn't have much longer to live, anyway.' He was right. It's true she was sick and old, but despite that, she lived alone, did her own grocery shopping, cleaned her house, washed her clothes, and took care of her finances.

"When that expert gave his description of my mother, he left something out. She was more than sick, old, and near death. She was a mother, grandmother, neighbor, and friend. Children adored her.

"Birds still line up on her fence in her front yard watching the door for her. She won't be there to feed her feathered friends pieces of bread every afternoon. She won't be around anymore to receive the Easter lilies, or the Easter baskets I made for her every year. All because a man she fed at her table, and who benefited from her kindness, decided to break into her home and rob her."

After I finished speaking, the judge asked the defendant to rise and imposed the maximum sentence on both counts, eight years on the burglary charge and ten years on the involuntary manslaughter charge. The sentences were consecutive, and the defendant was ordered to pay restitution and fines. But, I wasn't prepared for my reaction. Instead of elation, a sense of sadness swept over me.

Weeks after the trial, my mind kept going back to the man convicted for my mother's death. A security guard told me inmates who commit crimes against children and the elderly are given a rough time by other prisoners. My mother's trial generated a lot of publicity. I'm sure his identity was known when he arrived at the penitentiary.

Despite what he did to my mother, it didn't give me pleasure to think of him being mistreated in prison. Society's law demands punishment for offenses against its citizens. But, there's another law, a spiritual law. You reap what you sow. I knew, someday, he would experience what it felt like to be a victim.

Every time I think of him in a desolate prison cell, I say James Dillet Freeman's "Prayer for Protection" for him.

Talking to the police and detective assigned to the case during the trial gave me an opportunity to find out about the offender's background. He'd been in and out of prison several times. From all indication, he had a hard life. I saw him working in my mother's yard once. She introduced me to him. How strange to unknowingly meet the man responsible for your mother's death.

The detective told me about the defendant's addiction to crack cocaine.

"How could that be?" I asked. "He worked to earn money."

I will never forget his reply. "A crack addict will do anything to get crack — even work."

The infant who came out of his mother's womb wasn't a hardened criminal or violent crack addict. Something happened in life to change him. I wondered what events in childhood and throughout life caused him to turn out the way he did?

My stay on earth has been a picnic compared to his. How can I be sure that under similar circumstances I wouldn't have turned out the same way? A Cherokee prayer says, "Oh Great Spirit, grant that I may never find fault with my neighbor until I have walked the trail of life in his moccasins."

I had to force myself to stop dwelling on the unpleasantness of the past and look to the future. With the trial over, McDuff and I got back to the old routine. But, the old routine failed to satisfy me. I smelled change in the air.

Getting out of the legal field had been on my mind for a long time. My discontent and longing for something different prompted a change of jobs. I accepted an offer to work as a sales representative for an up-start company that sold natural gas over the Internet. The only bad part about the change was leaving all my friends at Vorys, but I knew we'd stick together. We always had.

I jokingly told them if this new company folded, I'd pack up and move to Las Vegas. Everyone knew how I loved to visit there. If I couldn't talk one of them into going with me, I'd fly to Sin City alone. Be careful of the words spoken in jest. They have a way of coming true. The company went under, but I received a job offer to work at the sister company. I thought about it for a few days.

"Nope, I am moving to Las Vegas," I told my boss. Just like that.

My buddies were flabbergasted when they learned of my decision, especially Marie.

"I'm moving to Las Vegas," I said as we sat at a booth eating lunch at Wendy's.

"You've got to be kidding. You're not serious," she said when I didn't reply. "Do you have a job lined up?"

"Nope."

"Do you have a place to live?"

"No, but I've been on the Internet checking out apartments."

"What are you going to do with your condo?"

"Sell it along with most of my possessions."

"Do you know anybody out there?"

"No, I don't."

"Judy, this is hard to believe. Are you sure you are making the right decision?"

"Remember that I told you if my new job didn't work out, I would move to Vegas."

We still laugh about the look of astonishment on her face when I told her of my plan over a hamburger and fries.

Telling Kelly didn't create the same consternation. No stranger to my impulsive acts, I believe if I told him I planned to jump off the Empire State Building, he'd offer to pack my parachute. I received a phone call from Pittsburgh two weeks after I informed him of my plans to move to Las Vegas. I knew he waited to see if I'd change my mind.

"Mom, I can't let you move all the way out there by yourself. I'm coming to Columbus to help with the move and get you settled in Nevada."

Even though I hadn't planned on his doing that, I'll be forever grateful. I had no idea of the magnitude of what I planned to undertake. He ended up staying four years. It's doubtful I could have made it on my own. Kelly is my rock.

Painful memories crowded around and suffocated me in Ohio. I believed moving out west with McDuff for a fresh start would clear the air. Look out, palm trees and desert sun, here we come!

## CHAPTER 9

# Go West, Young Scottie

*It takes a long time to grow an old friend.*
—JOHN LEONARD

EXCITEMENT MINGLED WITH A JOLT OF FEAR WHEN I THOUGHT ABOUT my decision to move to Nevada. Everything gained steam so fast that I barely had time to think — just dive in and flow with this tidal wave I started in motion.

A going-away party given by Trudy before I left Ohio took a strange and wonderful turn. The gathering of long-time friends will occupy a special place in my heart forever.

When the day of the party arrived, I welcomed the opportunity to escape from the mess and clutter created by packing. The chance to slow down and relax with my buddies at Trudy and David's beautiful, serene home fit my needs at the time.

Animated conversation floated through the air as I entered the house. Something had everyone buzzing with delight. I laughed when I found out what caused such excitement. They were each going to tell a "Judy story."

It became the party theme, and they had heard plenty of them. Every time I related a strange or amusing happening in my life, Trudy exclaimed, "It could only happen to Judy." Later, she and my Vorys friends shortened it to "only Judy." After I got McDuff, they began to clamor for "McDuff stories."

I told them to pick a favorite, and limited them to one story apiece. That created an uproar. We'd been friends and worked together at the law firm for many years. They felt restricting everyone to only one was unreasonable on my part.

"Come on, Judy. That's not fair. It's hard to decide on just one."

I didn't cave in under pressure. Each of them telling more would keep us there all night.

The dining room table overflowed with casseroles, salads, and other delicacies. The enticing aroma of chocolate-laden desserts caused my mouth to water as I strolled by the tempting selections. Everyone brought a dish we'd sampled and enjoyed at get-togethers through the years.

Friends sat on the plush, light-beige sectional sofa. Chairs lined the front of the fireplace and circled around the living room walls. The kids played games outside on the deck and in the large fenced-in back yard. With a house full of so many women, David soon made himself scarce.

My colleagues had become family. Even though some of us moved on to other jobs, we stayed in touch down through the years. Some of us boomeranged back after leaving the law firm. Another send-off party had been held for me when I left to attend The Ohio State University. They joked at that time, "Judy, this is your last going-away party."

Love, companionship, and sadness filled the room that sunny fall afternoon — laughter mixed with a healthy dose of tears. Friend after friend took turns telling their favorite tale. The room exploded in hysterics every time we heard what we all knew so well. They all ended by telling what our friendship meant to them, causing eyes to fill with tears.

Sitting in the place of honor in front of the picture window, I felt overcome with emotion. To top things off, they presented me with a substantial gift certificate from Target to buy things for my apartment in Nevada.

Finally, it was my turn to speak. I sat there for a moment in quiet contemplation while all eyes stared at me waiting for me to begin. Remembering, laughing, and crying with them made me realize something extraordinary had taken place in that room.

They didn't know that in my Will I specified I wanted a memorial service where all of my friends would gather and tell something funny about me. No sad, dreary funeral, only laughter and fun. After my amazement subsided, I began.

"You have just performed my memorial service while I am here on earth to see it."

I went on to tell them how fortunate and blessed I was to have so many true friends. How rare it is for people to stick together and stay connected the way we'd done through the years. Especially after some of us had moved on to other places of employment.

"We're family and we will always care and be concerned about each other. You've always encouraged and believed in me throughout all my hare-brained and impulsive schemes. I want you all to know how much I love, cherish, and will miss every one of you."

As I looked out over the smiling and tear-stained faces in the room, something struck me full force. A person is lucky to find one friend in life — I had been blessed with many. It would be hard to leave them, but I couldn't help myself. Something mysterious and deep down inside compelled me to move on. It couldn't be ignored.

The next day I threw myself back into preparing for the move. It's unbelievable how much stuff one accumulates in a house over the years. Deciding what to keep and what to sell created hours of agony. Unfortunately, when I finished, there was more on the "keep" side than on the "sell" side. I plowed through everything again and made more drastic cuts.

A valuable lesson about possessions came out of that move. I learned it wasn't the material things I wanted to hold on to. It was the sentiment attached to them I wanted to touch. I discovered that I didn't have to retain the material articles to keep the memories alive — the memories are safely stored away in my heart. The objects rust, fade, or crumble, but the mental picture of them remains for a lifetime in our minds.

Finally, the daunting task of affixing the price tags ended. With the help of Kelly and my dear friends, Marie, Jan, and

Vanessa, the moving sale began. Strangers milled around throughout the house and in the garage. McDuff flitted about checking out the happenings, greeting all the neighbors and people who came in and out.

He reveled in the activity and all the attention he received as people asked, "Is that a Scottish terrier?" He helped relieve my stress and lightened the tension as I watched him romp around. And, my friends eased the burden of having to dispose of so many of my personal belongings on my own.

The husband of a friend like Marie sure comes in handy when you decide to pack up and move across country. Harvey had worked for Lazarus Department Store in furniture delivery. He supervised and helped with loading the rental truck. I bet he never packed a fifteen-foot Ryder truck like a·can of sardines before. Even though I sold and gave away a mountain of my possessions, lots remained.

Every time he thought he'd put the last thing into the truck, I'd dash out of the door yelling, "Harvey, can we make room for this?" I'll never forget his patience with me that day or his expertise in getting so much into so little. I went to sleep weary, but satisfied in knowing we were packed and ready to roll.

I tossed and turned all night waiting for the alarm clock to go off. After last minute preparation in the morning, it was time to leave. Taking one last look around at my house and front yard, I bent over to smell my rose bush, fragrance dripping from its red velvet petals. How I hated leaving it behind.

My friend, Dolores, and her husband, Bill, came by to see us off. I gave Dolores my best umbrella, because *I wasn't going to need an umbrella in the desert.* That foolish act showed my lack of knowledge about monsoon season in southern Nevada. Some of the neighbors gathered around for final good-bye hugs and well wishes.

Just as we were pulling out, my buddy, Jan, sped up. "I'm so glad I got here in time to say good-bye," she said as we embraced.

Kelly and McDuff pulled away in the filled-to-the-brim truck. I drove behind them looking back in the rearview mirror of my car. Waving as long as I could see everybody, I drove into the future with what was left of my life packed into a rental truck.

September is a beautiful time of year in Ohio, bright skies and crisp air. But, I knew those grey, dreary days with dark clouds I hated lurked around the corner. A quick stop at U-Haul to pick up the auto transport and load my car on it, and we were on our way. The actual moment we hit the open road remains engraved in my memory to this day.

We drove on Interstate 70 heading west. McDuff sat on my lap with his head hanging out of the window, his long eyebrows and beard fluttering in the breeze. I had no idea at the time the creature sitting there would teach me valuable lessons about life on his mission in the desert. Sadness about what I'd left behind disappeared, and the anticipation of what lie ahead took its place.

I glanced over at Kelly. He's a professional truck driver, and driving is the passion of my son's life. A contented smile played on his lips as he gripped the steering wheel and focused on the highway in front of him. I could sense that he felt what I was experiencing. We welcomed the adventure of traveling across the United States together.

Journeying across country with a dog doesn't present a problem, anymore. I'd purchased a book that listed the motels that accepted pets. Kelly mapped out our route with that in mind. It nagged at me that McDuff might disturb others by barking in the motel rooms at night. I'd trained him to alert me upon hearing noises outside, because I lived alone.

Sure enough, the first night in Indianapolis, he heard someone walking past the room. Scrambling up, he raced to the door, barking all the way, while looking back at me. *Something's going on outside, but I got it covered.*

"That's enough," I said, his cue to stop.

Not long after that, a group of people walked by engaged in discussion and laughing wildly. Once again, McDuff charged across the room, challenging and threatening the strangers outside the door.

"That's enough, Duff. No!"

After that, he still went to the door and checked things out, but never created a disturbance again in the rooms.

Early in the morning, we set out for the next leg of our trip, Missouri. We hadn't been on the highway long before dark clouds threatened overhead, and the smell of rain filled the air. I felt a storm brewing. A torrential downpour tumbled from the clouds, accompanied by rumbling thunder. Lightning zigzagged across the sky. Seeing more than a few feet in front of the truck became impossible.

My throat tightened and my stomach knotted as the truck crept along. Driving in bad weather didn't scare Kelly. It's part of the job to him. Terror gripped me as a blast of wind jerked the truck and attached auto transport out of our lane. Traffic whizzed by splashing up sheets of water making visibility worse. McDuff slept peacefully at his spot on the floor between my feet, oblivious to it all. Unlike most dogs, thunderstorms never bothered him in the least.

Scared as I was though, I had complete faith in Kelly's ability to handle the situation. It also helped to know rainstorms in that part of the country stop as suddenly as they start. Sure enough, the rain turned into a light drizzle, then ceased. Clouds parted to reveal blue skies and sunshine. At last, full speed ahead on the road to Missouri. Except for an expected speed bump caused by my kidneys on the way there.

Many family stories exist about my notoriously weak kidneys. The fright from that fierce storm had taken its toll on them.

"Kelly, I need to make a pit stop, the sooner the better."

"I saw a sign for a roadside rest stop ahead," he said with a knowing laugh.

"Oh, great." Catastrophe averted — or so I thought.

I failed to take into consideration traveling in a truck with a car in tow meant not pulling in the space reserved for cars in front of the restroom. We would have to find a spot in the truck parking area. With tractor trailers hogging parking spaces everywhere, it took a while.

After we parked, I sprang out of the door and started toward the ladies room at a trot that quickly turned into a scissor walk.

The toilet was far away from the truck area — way too far. My bladder threatened to burst at any moment.

Kelly sensed my apprehension as he walked away with McDuff.

"You going to make it, Mom?" he called out over his shoulder.

"I don't know. Keep your fingers crossed," I replied through clinched teeth with alarm bells going off in my head.

My destination could have been in China for all it mattered. I knew I couldn't make it. The thought of public humiliation is never a welcome visitor, but it was getting ready to drop in and make itself at home. I had a choice — wet my pants or come up with an ego-saving alternative fast.

As I pee-pee stepped by a wooden cabin sitting on a concrete slab, I saw a forest ranger in a brown uniform through the window. He wrote at a wooden desk unaware of my spying. A tall, green metal trash barrel sat beside the building. A feeling of relief shot through my mind. *Just the cover I need!* I ducked behind it and peered through the bottom of the window pane to make sure the ranger hadn't seen me. Then, my eyes swept the surrounding area. The coast was clear.

My bladder deflated for what seemed like fifteen minutes. I heard the sound of the ranger's chair scrap the floor as he got up to move around the room. My eyes widened. I crouched down lower. *Please don't let him see me,* I thought in desperation. He didn't. Luckily, no one else from the roadside rest did either. Mission accomplished.

I nonchalantly emerged from behind the barrel, smoothed my clothes, and blended in with the other travelers. Arriving back at the truck, I relayed my escapade to Kelly. He slapped his sides and howled as I described my reaction when the ranger got up.

"Mom, this is the best kidney story yet," he said between peals of laughter.

After spending the night in Jefferson City, Missouri, we set out for Oklahoma, our next stop on the map. We traveled on scenic Route 66 for a while. As we drove further into the state of Oklahoma, the truck began to slow down, and then crawled along. Even though we drove on a flat, level highway, the gears whined and shifted continuously.

Kelly had the gas pedal to the floor, but it refused to go any faster. My nerves flared as my mind flashed back to Ohio. *Why did I insist on putting so much stuff on this truck? It's getting ready to break down out here in the middle of nowhere.*

I looked out of the window and noticed something peculiar. The trees and shrubbery beside the highway were bending and twisting wildly. Kelly saw it, too.

"Mom, I think I know why the truck is so slow. Look at the trees."

I nodded, relieved to know it was the wind and not the overloaded truck creating the slowdown.

Before long, we reached a toll booth and watched a tattered flag snapping in the blustery breeze above it.

"You're driving straight into a headwind," the operator said. "It's going to be slow going for you for a while." She sure knew what she was talking about.

We drove across the Texas Panhandle after spending the night in Elk City, Oklahoma. Up until now, McDuff handled the trip well. I began to sense his attitude changing. After stops, he took his good time climbing back into the truck. The first sign of Scottie discontent began to surface. It would soon erupt into a full-blown rebellion.

The terrain changed drastically in New Mexico, brown, dry, and desert looking. The lack of grass created an equation for McDuff — no grass equals no poop. Each time we stopped for him to relieve himself, he'd search for that nonexistent grassy spot.

"Poop, Duff," I urged motioning to a spot on the arid ground. *Are you kidding? No way! What happened to the grass?*

We started stopping along the highway like prospectors searching for gold. No luck, not even a small patch. He held it for a couple of days before we stopped at a barren roadside rest. Kelly walked away with him while I went to the ladies room. As I came out, I saw Kelly running toward me yelling, his hand waving wildly overhead as he dragged McDuff along behind him.

"Grass, Mom, grass. He pooped! He pooped!"

Of course, everyone around looked at him like he was crazy. But, they didn't know how much that small, pathetic patch of grass helped us out. I understood and shared in his exhilaration. McDuff was the happiest of all, and much lighter since he hadn't done number two since Texas.

We stayed in Albuquerque that night and set out for Flagstaff, Arizona the next morning. McDuff dragged himself out of the motel on the morning of the fifth day of the trip with no bounce whatsoever in his step. After two or three attempts to jump up into the high truck, he wearily plopped his rear down on the ground.

"Come on, Duff. You can make it one more day. We're almost there. Please, get in," I coaxed him. I knew if we didn't reach our destination soon, we'd have a mutiny on our hands.

The last leg of the trip took us through Hoover Dam. I couldn't believe what I saw as we approached. A narrow two-lane road snaked down to the dam with tourists walking in front and behind traffic, cameras in hand. We inched along stealing glances at what we could see of the magnificent structure.

Once we drove by it, all we had to do was navigate the steep road out of the dam area. Because we slowed down to avoid hitting the sightseers, the truck couldn't muster up enough speed. It chugged up the hill like that little engine in one of my favorite childhood stories. "I think I can, I think I can, I think I can."

"Kelly, we're not going to make it," I said, holding my breath as the truck clawed its way to the top.

I imagined the truck and auto transport sliding backward sending tourists flying through the air like bowling pins into Hoover Dam.

"Relax, Mom. We'll make it."

As we inched along for what seemed like forever, the top of the hill came into sight. I exhaled, and started to breathe normally again. Henderson was just a few miles away. Poor McDuff's ordeal would soon be over. Or, so we thought.

We rolled into our apartment complex in mid-afternoon weary and worn. I'd made a visit earlier in the year to check it out, and discovered it lovelier than I remembered. Green shrubbery loaded with pink and lavender blooms, lots of grass, and flower beds with my favorite flowers from back east, petunias and pansies. Tall palm trees swayed around the swimming pool — a real oasis in the desert.

After we left the rental office, Kelly found a place large enough to park. As we approached our apartment building, we confronted eighteen steps of concrete mixed with small colored stones. The ground below showed through the space between each one. Sturdy green railing on each side provided support. *They're high, but McDuff won't have a problem climbing them,* I thought. Wrong. He refused to budge.

*What kind of crazy steps are these? No way am I climbing all the way up there. The trip out here was bad enough, but this is the last straw.*

"Come on, Duff. Let's go, Boy. You can do it," I pleaded.

After about ten minutes of playing good cop, bad cop with him, I knew that headstrong Scottie of mine had no intention of climbing that high, strange-looking flight of stairs.

"Let's carry him up," Kelly said, ready to get inside and unwind. "He'll do it on his own the next time."

We carried that pudgy canine up and down those steps three times a day for a week before he reluctantly decided to do it on his own. Years later I would remember the way he fought those stairs that day.

I believe we went to the desert for McDuff to teach me things I needed to learn about life. We would meet individuals at Project PRIDE on his mission out west. Because of them, McDuff taught me to change the way I looked at and judged others.

## CHAPTER 10

# Project PRIDE at
# Opportunity Village

*Judge not according to the appearance,*
*but judge righteous judgment.*
—JOHN 7:24 (KING JAMES VERSION)

O PENING THE DOOR BY THE PROJECT PRIDE SIGN, I ENTERED THE
room with McDuff trotting at my side. *Oh my God!* My
heart beat faster as I looked around the room. *What have
you gotten yourself into?* I thought, and almost stopped in my
tracks. *Don't panic. Be calm and hang around for a little while.
Then, you can get out of here. You can't just turn around and
leave now.*

The caretakers' eyes watched my reaction with veiled interest. They'd seen therapy dog volunteers like me come and go
before. McDuff pranced around my feet, tail wagging, while
tugging on the leash anxious to meet potential new admirers.

He dragged me over to the nearest person for attention. "Is
he a Scottish terrier?" one of them asked while petting him.
After the initial distraction caused by our intrusion, everyone
proceeded with their activities before the interruption.

Moving to an out-of-the-way spot, I looked closer at the
boys and girls in the large, bright room with floor to ceiling
windows on one side. A kitchen area against the wall contained a sink, refrigerator, countertop with small appliances,

and stove. I noticed a rocking chair, dinette set, video, and medical equipment.

Toys were scattered throughout the room. The brightly colored walls danced with cartoon characters and other things designed to stimulate the attention of children.

One boy strapped upright to a high tilted board ate baby food spooned to him by a caretaker. A small blonde girl about three or four years-old scooted around on the floor behind an enclosed area in one corner of the room. Suspended above the floor in a swing-like device, a slender, dark-haired boy hung with a tube to a food pump connected to his stomach.

Another girl I estimated to be a teenager with short black hair sat at a table in a wheelchair. Her large eyes followed us with growing apprehension. A tiny boy lay motionless on his back on an elevated bed placed against the wall.

Then, it hit me — the total silence in the room. Except for the girl on the floor, none of the others moved around or made a sound. *How in the world am I expected to perform therapy dog work with this group?* I grew more anxious to leave with every passing moment.

Since no one seemed to pay me any attention, I began to walk around the room to get a closer look. I took care to keep McDuff and his leash out of the way. He glanced from one kid to the other, puzzled by their lack of attention to him.

The eyes of some of them were unfocused and unseeing. I later learned they were described as individuals having the most severe mental and physical disabilities in the state of Nevada. And, to my surprise, they were not boys and girls, but young adults in their early to mid-twenties.

Completely unnerved, at a loss at what to do next, I checked out McDuff and observed him glancing from one person to the next. He pulled on his leash and guided me around the room. I followed him over to the young man strapped to the tilt table and started a conversation with the woman feeding him.

"His name is Chris. He can't walk, talk, see, or use his arms. He wears diapers," she told me.

Since Chris was so far off the floor, I picked McDuff up to bring him closer. Not knowing what to expect next, I watched McDuff's unwavering stare at Chris — that same strange stare he gave me at the kennel when I first picked him up. After several minutes, McDuff bent over, and tenderly began licking Chris on the face.

Something unusual about the licking struck me right away. It wasn't the typical way I'd seen him lick others. Soft, deliberate, focused, and much slower, his tongue stroked Chris's cheek. That's when something unexpected happened that shocked us all — Chris smiled.

"Come here, quick! Chris is smiling!" the woman shouted out to her colleagues, almost dropping the jar of baby food in her hand. They rushed over to us amazed, eyes wide in astonishment, as they watched Chris and McDuff in their own private world. They told me that Chris never reacted to anything by smiling before.

Perhaps, the way McDuff licked Chris' cheek with his soft, warm tongue conveyed an entirely different sensation, one that he had never experienced before. Or, maybe, it was something else — McDuff's acceptance and unconditional love coming through.

I realized, perhaps, I didn't know what to do here, or how to react, but McDuff did. He saw beyond outer appearances and didn't hesitate to offer unconditional acceptance. I knew then we would return to Project PRIDE for him to provide more comfort and joy in his own special way.

That's how we discovered Opportunity Village's Project PRIDE (People's Rights to Independence, Dignity and Equality). It's a nationally recognized program that offers parents relief from the stress of round-the-clock medical and personal care for family members who need constant attention. Opportunity Village is Nevada's largest private, nonprofit community rehabilitation program, and is well known in Sin City as "Las Vegas' Favorite Charity."

After the initial shock of my first visit, we began once a week morning visits for a couple of hours. That didn't last. Before long, we were going two and three times a week and staying until the last person left in the early afternoon.

Afterward, I had to literally drag McDuff, his four paws stubbornly planted on the pavement, across the parking lot to the car. Once there, he refused to get in. I had to lift that stiff, stocky canine into the car. His disapproving glare made it clear to me he wasn't ready to go as I drove home. And, this happened after every visit.

Charlotte, the supervisor, and Angela, Maria, and Eric were the best caretakers in the world. The love and attention they gave the clients, as they were called, warmed my heart. As I watched them provide care dipped in tenderness and love, I realized what a special breed of people they were.

I tried to keep out of the way with McDuff as they moved around taking care of everyone, but it proved difficult. One therapy dog volunteer rule is that your dog must be kept on a leash at all times. That rule soon fell by the wayside by mutual agreement after the first few visits.

It was too awkward getting around everyone, the equipment, and furniture in the room. I felt confident taking him off leash wouldn't cause a problem. He savored his new-found freedom. He could hang out around the kitchen on his own and get goodies at lunch time. Still, the separate room used to change diapers and perform clean ups remained off limits.

I brought some of McDuff's toys from home so he would leave the toys that belonged to the clients alone. He complied for the most part. But, even a well-trained therapy dog couldn't resist temptation when it came to Kathy's Elmo.

Little Kathy couldn't walk or talk, and wore diapers. But, she had use of her arms, limited vision, and wasn't connected to a feeding pump. Scooting on the floor in a partitioned-off corner of the room gave her mobility. She looked like a little girl, but looks were deceiving. All of the residents there appeared to be children, because their infirmities prevented them from developing normally.

Kathy loved being held and rocked in the rocking chair while she snuggled in someone's arms and held Elmo. Playing in her little corner of the world made her happy and content, too.

McDuff jumped into her cordoned-off area to play with her, but he had an ulterior motive. Sure, she had neat things to play with in there that caught his eye. And, something else he desired in the worst way — big-eyed, bright-red Elmo from Sesame Street.

Kathy had to hold her favorite toy a few inches from her eyes to see him, but Elmo touched something in her. He touched something in McDuff, too — greed and envy. That dog tried to steal Elmo from her every chance he got.

At first he simply took it. "McDuff, drop it!" I'd shout out from across the room. After the first few unsuccessful attempts, he realized stealing Elmo wouldn't be easy. That's when the buried criminal instinct kicked in. "Slick" McDuff came out like Mr. Hyde; Dr. Jekyll, the heroic, dedicated therapy dog, receded into the background. At least once a visit he launched a clandestine raid to sneak off with Elmo.

He had a strike against him, though. That "walk" I came to know after he stole something tipped me off every time. Even with his back to me, and when I couldn't see Elmo in his mouth, I'd command, "Drop it, Duff," as he tried to slink out of sight. Out tumbled Elmo, to be returned to a bewildered and grateful Kathy once more.

I know Kathy never figured out what that short, black, hairy thing was that occupied her space at times. But never mind that. She soon learned to protect Elmo from it.

While talking to Charlotte one day, I failed to keep an eye on what transpired in Kathy's corner of the room. I heard a commotion and looked up just in time to see McDuff latched onto Elmo, and poor Kathy holding on for dear life. A fierce tug of war ensued. From all appearances, McDuff was gaining ground.

"McDuff, NO!" He let go right away and directed his attention elsewhere as though he couldn't understand how Elmo got into his mouth. I knew it was an act. That Scottie burglar didn't fool me for one minute. He had no intention of giving up.

When Christmas arrived that year, Santa put a big, red Elmo under the tree for McDuff. Now, he had an Elmo all his own. Oh, he still launched raids to get Elmo from Kathy, but the intensity diminished. He concentrated on the relationship he developed with Nathaniel.

Nathaniel, though mostly confined to the hanging device, sometimes lay on a floor mat, or sat in a wheelchair. Unlike the other clients, Nathaniel had limited communication skills and could raise his arms to indicate "yes" or "no." I must admit he became my favorite client. His face lit up like afternoon sunshine on a desert landscape whenever he spotted us walking toward him.

McDuff and Nathaniel played a game that they both loved, fetch the ball. While Nathaniel lay on the floor, I'd place a ball in his hand, and with a slight flutter of his wrist, the ball crawled across the floor. McDuff retrieved the ball and dropped it by his hand to repeat the toss.

Quite often there wasn't enough oomph on the ball to propel it forward, and it rolled behind Nathaniel's head instead of in front of him. That didn't matter. McDuff raced behind him and picked it up.

Things really got lively when Nathaniel sat in his wheelchair and "threw" the ball. Throwing meant letting the ball roll down the front of his body which caused it to go faster and roll further across the floor.

Nathaniel couldn't hide his excitement and delight. He didn't get tired of throwing the ball, and his buddy, McDuff, didn't get tired of retrieving it. They made a perfect match.

Here's the kicker about McDuff and playing fetch. With me on our walks in the park, I'd throw his tennis ball as far as I could and tell him to fetch it. Off he streaked on those low-to-the-ground legs, chase down the ball, and return it to me to throw again. After he brought it back three or four times, I'd throw it and say, "Fetch."

McDuff sat down on the grass and looked up at me without budging. *I'm finished. Now, you fetch it.* "McDuff, fetch the ball!" I ordered, pointing and stomping my foot for emphasis. *You must be out of your mind. I'm tired, get it yourself.*

No threat or command from me compelled him to retrieve it once he had enough. Of course, it was an entirely different story with his friend, Nathaniel. But then, he didn't have to go as far to retrieve it. Guess that made the difference. Nathaniel enjoyed playing with McDuff, but Naomi wanted no part of him.

We frightened Naomi on our first visit to the program. She knew we were strangers, and it intimidated her. I pulled up a chair beside her wheelchair with McDuff sitting on my lap. She stiffened and turned her back to us, glancing over her shoulder in short intervals to see if McDuff was still there. Curiosity overcame her. *What kind of black, furry thing is this beside me?* she wondered.

Her glances away became fewer, her posture softened, and she began to smile at him. Once more, I observed the eerie stare from McDuff as he watched her. He didn't try to lick her as he had the others. Without moving, he just sat there with those dark eyes never leaving her face.

I began talking to Naomi, telling her about McDuff in an attempt to put her at ease. She jerked around and faced him. With an ornery smile, her thumb and forefinger darted out and grasped and pulled one of those protruding Scottish terrier eyebrows. Since I held him on my lap with both hands, I was unable to intervene.

He sat unmoving and unflinching as her fingers came closer and closer to his eye. I'd seen him do the same thing another time when a three-year-old child darted up to him, stooped over, and pulled both his eyebrows. Naomi pulled McDuff's eyebrows, beard, and long pointed ears with glee every time she saw him. Unfortunately, not all the clients were able to interact with him.

Other than Chris, Matthew exhibited the most severe disabilities. I wish we could have connected with him. He lay on his bed not moving most of the time, although he followed us with his eyes. Watching videos seemed to pacify him. McDuff provided generous licks to the cheek when we visited, even though Matthew didn't react to them. However, McDuff had another place to go in the building and be the center of attention.

A warehouse in the back of the building called the Work Center provided employment for about seventy individuals with intellectual disabilities, many with Down's Syndrome. They shredded documents, assembled condiment packets, and performed other contracted jobs. Everyone worked while sitting in folding chairs at long tables.

McDuff visited the Work Center to the delight and amusement of the clients there. It became a momentous event for them, and brought an air of excitement to their daily routine. Whenever we arrived, cheers rang out. A chorus of "I want to pet the dog," and "Bring him over here by me," erupted throughout the warehouse.

They weren't permitted to get out of their chairs, so McDuff went around the entire room and sat for each client to pet and talk to him. It took quite a while. Joy and delight shone on every face as hands reached out to pat McDuff's head and rub his back. It made their day and ours, too.

We didn't get to the Work Center during every visit to Project PRIDE because of the amount of time it took, but we relished our visits there. Every facet of therapy dog work at Opportunity Village flowed like a calm mountain stream. But, rapids raged ahead.

Maybe I was naïve. It never entered my mind that not all of our special friends would be there when McDuff and I visited each week. Sure, I knew of their life-threatening medical problems requiring around-the-clock attention, and how fragile they were. Still, their fighting spirits enabled them to bounce back from a crisis time after time.

Seeing how they struggled and persevered every moment of their lives made them strong in my sight. How could I let something like a head cold or sinus problems get me down? By the very act of breathing, they became my inspiration. One day the inevitable happened, and it caught me completely off guard.

I noticed Chris' absence and the different atmosphere the moment we entered the room. No one made eye contact with me as I greeted everyone. Sadness filled the air like dense smoke.

"Where's Chris?" I asked, looking around the room for him. No one answered at first. I looked at Maria, then Angela, and finally, Eric as they made themselves busy attending to the others. A sinking feeling crept into the pit of my stomach.

"Judy, Chris' mom didn't bring him earlier this week because of complications," Charlotte finally answered. "She called and told us yesterday that he didn't make it this time."

My heart skipped a beat. *Chris didn't make it?* Tears burned my eyes. My mind went blank. Charlotte saw how hard it hit me.

"Just let it out," she said taking me in her arms. When I finally pulled myself together, she explained what happened to Chris, and gave me details of the funeral arrangements.

Everyone hugged me before I left. In their profession, they learn how to deal with death and protect themselves. My emotions tossed and turned like a canoe shooting over a waterfall. I needed to take a lesson from them, and fast, if I wanted to stay afloat at Project PRIDE.

I had no idea how deeply Chris' death would affect me. It may be hard for those with no experience with the disabled to understand. After all, how could someone as horribly impaired as Chris get to you? Well, I can tell you this: There was a light deep inside of him that sparkled and shined through all the damage. Even his smallest achievement became everyone's victory. His sweet, courageous, and accepting demeanor made you jump up and root for him.

Most of all, his life made you aware of how fortunate and blessed you were; you could not take anything in your life for granted. Yes, something in Chris touched us all. His funeral testified to that.

I drove around the parking lot at Bunkers Mortuary amazed by all the cars packed in every available parking space. There must be another funeral being held at the same time, I thought. It took me a while to find a place to park.

Walking into the funeral home, I encountered wall-to-wall people. I spotted Charlotte and the group from Project PRIDE. Moving through the crowd with difficulty, I inched my way over to them.

"This place is really packed. Who are all these people?" I asked.

"They're Chris' family, friends, co-workers of the family, and members of his church," Charlotte answered.

We filed into the chapel for the funeral service. What I experienced there will remain with me for a lifetime. Person after person walked to the front of the chapel and talked about Chris and the devotion, and tender, loving care shown to him by his mother. How she cared for him day after day, uncomplaining and positive, even after it adversely affected her health. They told of the way Chris' spirit touched them and somehow made them better people.

Chris' brother shared how one day everything went wrong on his job. He fought the bumper-to-bumper, slow moving traffic to get home afterward. By the time he pulled into the driveway, frazzled, frustrated, and in a rotten mood, he stormed into the house. The first person he saw was his brother.

"Hi, Chris," he said. As he watched his brother's face light up at his greeting, it hit him hard. Nothing he had endured that day mattered at all. Seeing Chris made him ashamed of his pity party; seeing Chris made him thankful and aware of his blessings.

Crying so hard when I left the funeral home, and too emotionally distressed to drive on the freeway, I took the side streets home. When I arrived, McDuff rushed up to greet me.

I sat down on the floor with him to tell him all about the funeral of his buddy, and that he wouldn't see Chris on his next visit to Project PRIDE. With each mention of Chris' name, McDuff's long, pointed ears flickered. He sat in front of me with his eyes burning deep into mine as I spoke.

I thanked him for coming into my life and teaching me how to love, accept, and look to the inside of people. Not to judge by what I saw on the outside. I told him he helped me become a better person. That he saw beyond appearances and accepted Chris, Kathy, Nathaniel, Naomi, Matthew, and all the clients in the Work Center, unconditionally from the first moment. I let him know that he had detected in them what I'd been unable to see.

Although McDuff was way ahead of me, I came to see, accept, and love them in the same way; another one of the life lessons I learned from McDuff on our journey together.

Somehow, McDuff's therapy dog work at Project PRIDE came to the attention of the media. KVBC Channel 3 TV News in Las Vegas sent a reporter and crew to do a special feature on him. Opportunity Village's switchboard at its headquarters jammed from the large volume of calls received the day it played.

An operator called for permission to give my telephone number to callers who wanted information about McDuff and the therapy dog program. I talked to many people informing them how to get involved with their dogs.

The *Anthem View* newspaper featured him on the front page with the caption, "MCDUFF IS ON THE JOB." Articles ran in other Henderson newspapers and on the Internet. On walks in the park, at the veterinarian's office, or anywhere I took him, people approached and asked, "Is his name McDuff?"

He became a celebrity, and he enjoyed every minute. However, circumstances beyond my control would separate us from the clients at Project PRIDE and leave a hole in our lives.

It pained me to make the decision to accept a job offer. I hadn't worked since I arrived in September 2000. At some point I knew that I'd have to find a full-time job. I knew the work schedule would probably conflict with Project PRIDE's hours, making it impossible to continue going there weekdays with McDuff.

The staff had become my friends. We went to the Opportunity Village Christmas party, birthday parties, and shows on the Las Vegas Strip together.

"Guys, you know that job I told you I interviewed for at the Clark County Courthouse in Las Vegas? Well, I got it. I start next week," I said, enveloped in sadness instead of joy.

We sat silent for a while. One by one, they assured me they understood, but we all knew deep down inside something special was coming to an end. McDuff and I went back to visit whenever I had a day off from work during the week, which seldom occurred.

Now, we concentrated on evening nursing home visits and weekend rounds at St. Rose Dominican Hospitals. We also went to assisted living facilities. I sensed McDuff's bewilderment when we stopped going to Project PRIDE. I knew he missed Nathaniel, Kathy, Naomi, and Matthew just as much as I did.

Our journey had not ended. It came to a fork in the road. Opportunities lay ahead for McDuff to teach me more of his valuable life lessons. A boy named Steven would meet McDuff on the path, and that meeting changed his life forever.

## CHAPTER 11

# Reading with McDuff

*Animals are such agreeable friends.*
*They ask no questions, they pass no criticisms.*
—GEORGE ELIOT

GOING BACK TO WORK AND LEAVING OUR FRIENDS AT PROJECT PRIDE left a void. I felt guilty about McDuff being alone most of the day. Even though Kelly got off from his job earlier than me and walked him, it didn't ease my conscience.

We visited nursing homes in the evening, but not on a regular basis because of the demands of my employment at the courthouse. The empty space in our lives became full with Steven, a chubby, sandy-haired fifth grader, and the Reading with Rover Program.

Mary at K-9 Therapists of Las Vegas knew of my dilemma. Working full time during the week made it impossible to take McDuff on therapy dog visits. I was delighted to receive a call from her telling me about a new and innovative program beginning at the Paseo Verde Library called Reading with Rover. She thought I'd be interested because the sessions were on Saturday mornings.

"Call Florica at the library and ask her to give you more information. It's something new and different from the other therapy dog things," she advised.

I called her, arranged a meeting, and took McDuff with me to the library. Florica impressed me immensely at our first meeting. Slender, with dark hair and a radiant smile, the love for children sparkled in her eyes as she told me about the program's positive impact on students with reading problems. She and McDuff hit it off right away. *This sounds like the thing for us,* I thought listening intently.

She told me the program would pair certified therapy dogs with students from grades one through five in a nonjudgmental environment. They would meet once a week in the Children's Library reading room. Kids, who were uncomfortable reading aloud in front of others in the classroom, or struggling with reading, would be nominated by their parents, teachers, or caregivers. Need and space available determined the selection.

McDuff and three other dogs would initiate the program at the library. If the program proved successful, she planned to expand it.

"You and McDuff will be in the room with a student. No one else is allowed in during the session," Florica said. "Don't interfere or assist the child unless asked, and then, answer only what is asked of you. After the session, be sure to give lots of praise and encouragement."

Reading with Rover's goal is to elevate low self-esteem and improve reading skills. The bond developed between students and the dogs would make reading to the dogs fun without the fear of criticism. The dogs provide unconditional acceptance and support; they don't judge.

All types and sizes of therapy dogs are acceptable in the program. They must pass an obedience test, exhibit excellent temperaments, and have a love of children.

Florica provided the nomination form submitted by Steven's mother. His mother had checked the boxes indicating that Steven struggled with reading, found reading frustrating, and was participating in a special reading class at school.

She wrote in the comment section that Steven's problem with reading affected the rest of his studies, especially math word problems. His love of dogs and animals prompted her to jump at the chance to have him considered for the program.

Excitement tingled up and down my spine. I looked forward to this new adventure with McDuff. From past experience, I knew nothing ordinary happened where he was concerned. I grew to expect unusual occurrences, and he didn't disappoint me. But, the impact he would have on Steven's life was beyond my wildest imagination.

I met Steven and his mother at the library before the first session. He gave me a shy grin when we were introduced. His eyes lit up at the sight of McDuff bounding over to greet him like welcoming a long-lost member of the pack.

Susan, a petite, attractive woman with short blonde hair, stood by watching them with a smile on her face. Steven and McDuff bonded on the spot, and the bond grew stronger with each passing week.

The bright, cheery Story Room at the Paseo Verde Library was approximately 15 feet by 20 feet with a blue and gold tiled floor. A blue carpeted border provided a perfect place to sit and lean back against the wall while reading. The Children's Courtyard seen through the large sliding glass door on one side of the room provided a connection to the outdoors.

A sink and counter jutted out from one wall, and a long table placed against the opposite wall was lined with children's books. The room yelled out to the kids passing by, "Come in and have a good time reading!"

A chair discreetly placed against the wall awaited me. I chatted with Steven about his interests while he picked through the large assortment of books. Surprisingly, I found his taste similar to mine — animals and nature. Thank goodness, because I'd wondered how boring the session might be just sitting there. Steven's choice of books would hold my interest for the forty-five minute session.

Our first Reading with Rover session began. Steven sat cross-legged on a rose colored blanket placed on the carpet. McDuff sat in front of him. Steven began reading aloud. McDuff watched Steven's face, puzzled, because he thought Steven was talking to him. After a while, he realized that wasn't the case.

He turned toward me and our eyes met. *What's going on here? Am I supposed to just sit here and do nothing?* I remained silent on my out-of-the-way chair against the wall. He stood up, looked around the room, and started to walk away.

"No, Duff. Sit! Stay!" I ordered. He sat down and never again attempted to walk away while Steven read. Week after week, McDuff sat and listened with those long, erect Scottie ears. Florica later remarked after observing him in the Reading Room, "McDuff's more serious than the other dogs. He seems to know this is important."

Some of the kids said their dogs were silly, stepped on their books, tried to lick them while they read, fell asleep, or didn't listen. Not McDuff. He was all business, and he demonstrated just how seriously he took his job one Saturday morning when he got kicked out of the library.

We arrived a little early for our eleven a.m. session. I found the room occupied by the Reading with Rover team scheduled ahead of us. As I looked through the window into the room, McDuff stood in front of the door anticipating my opening it to let him in the room.

When that didn't happen, he began to scratch on the door. Then, he barked fast and furiously all the while looking at me. *What's wrong with you? Open the door so we can get started.*

Mortified, I tried to quiet him. He was having no part of it. He wanted in, and didn't intend to shut up until I opened the door and let him in. I can assure you a dog barking in a library draws lots of attention, fast. Florica flew out of her office to check on the commotion.

"He wants to go into the reading room right now," I whispered to her while trying to drag this disturber of the peace away from the door. The people in the Children's Library section gathered around. Soon, patrons arrived from every section of the library.

"Judy, you'll have to remove him from the library until he settles down," Florica whispered.

"Steven, take him outside right away!" I said thrusting the red leash into his hands.

Steven doubled over with laughter, and Florica watched us, amused. Embarrassed by the curious people standing around gawking, I failed to see the humor.

Steven tugged the resisting, boisterous McDuff away from the door, and dragged him outside. I overheard a white-haired lady say to her husband, "See, I told you. I'm not crazy. I did hear a dog barking."

"From now on, when I get here before our time, I'll keep him outside," I told Florica while breathing a sigh of relief. And that's what I did.

The connection between Steven and McDuff was noticeably different from the other therapy dog pairings. Steven sensed McDuff's interest in him, and that he really listened to him read. When Steven tired halfway through the session, he'd say to me, "Judy, McDuff is tired. I'm going to walk him around the room." After one or two laps, they resumed their positions, and Steven continued on with the session.

Remaining seated on my chair, I became invisible to them, because they had their own thing going on. Whenever I heard Steven mispronounce or stumble over a word, I remained silent. Unexpectedly, one morning, Steven asked, "Judy, how do you say this word?" I walked over to him, looked at the page, and pronounced it for him. After that, he regularly asked me, but I was careful to answer only what he asked me and nothing else.

The six weeks flew by, and the session ended. Steven received a diploma. We received a Certificate of Appreciation from the Henderson District Public Library. Steven and McDuff appeared on television with the other participants promoting the program.

In the *Las Vegas Sun* newspaper article, "Reading Goes to the Dogs," Florica referred to McDuff as "a Scottish terrier with attitude." It was time for Steven to move on to the next session and pair up with another dog. He rebelled. No way was he going to be parted from McDuff.

One night I received a phone call from a distraught Susan. "Judy, Steven is upset and crying his eyes out. He says he won't continue with another therapy dog. He wants to stay with McDuff.

I talked to Florica, but she says the rules are the children must rotate with other therapy dogs. Please talk to her, and see if she will make an exception for him just this one time."

"I've been expecting your call," Florica said when she heard my voice.

We discussed the strong bond between Steven and McDuff and how remarkably his grades, reading, and self-esteem had improved during the past six weeks. She relented.

"I'll make an exception and give Steven another session with McDuff, but only one more time. I'll call Susan and tell her."

I knew Susan would be ecstatic to hear the good news. But, she, Florica, and I didn't know that McDuff wasn't finished with Steven. Destiny brought them together for a greater purpose.

Steven's grandmother knew how his grades improved because of the program and reading to McDuff. She announced that she was coming to the library to see for herself on Saturday. She observed her grandson and McDuff through the one-way glass window to the reading room. As we ended the session and exited the room, I saw her standing outside shaking her head from side to side.

"I can't believe my eyes. That dog sat in one place for forty-five minutes and listened to Steven read. It's amazing," I heard her say to Susan.

The second and final six-week session for Steven with McDuff ended. I received a phone call from an excited Susan.

"Judy, I can't believe this! Steven made the honor roll for the first time," she said in an escalating voice.

After two sessions of reading with McDuff, Steven went from a "D" average to the honor roll. All of the children in the program showed improvement in reading skills to some degree, but this was far above normal.

Susan told me, at the honor roll ceremony at his school, some of the other students asked Steven how he went from "Ds" to the honor roll. "It's because of McDuff and Judy," he proudly exclaimed. Susan told them about the Reading with Rover Program, and the Scottish terrier therapy dog responsible for

Steven's mind-blowing advancement. Contact between Steven and McDuff didn't end after the second session.

Sleepovers at Steven's house started innocently enough. During the second session, as we waited outside the library for Steven's mother to pick him up, the conversation turned to how much he wanted a dog of his own.

"Steven, how about McDuff spending a weekend at your house after the session ends? Maybe your parents will change their minds about letting you have a dog."

A big smile lit up his face as he asked breathlessly, "Do you think that would work?"

We spent the rest of the time plotting like two pirates. When Susan arrived, we both greeted her with conspiratorial smirks. One evening my phone rang.

"Steven wants me to ask if McDuff can come over to his house next weekend. We'll pick him up on Saturday and bring him back on Sunday if that's alright with you."

What started out as a weekend sleepover mushroomed. Before long, McDuff had a dog dish, water bowl, toys, and supply of dog food at Steven's house.

Susan e-mailed me photos of McDuff participating in family activities. One showed Amy, Steven's adorable little sister, and her little playmates with him. Their petite, shining faces arranged around his like delicate petals on a black-eyed Susan. All you could see of McDuff was his black nose in the center.

Susan told me, when bedtime arrived on the first weekend, Steven took him into his bedroom to spend the night. That didn't work. McDuff kept leaving and going into Susan's bedroom. I knew the reason. He was used to sleeping in my bedroom in the bed with me. Steven enticed him back, and shut the door.

McDuff sat there shooting glances at Steven to open it and let him out. Finally, the problem was solved. The entire family slept in sleeping bags on the living room floor with McDuff that night.

McDuff received royal treatment at Steven's house. Nothing was too good for him. One afternoon at a family cookout, I watched Steven's dad, Dave, cook a medium-rare hamburger pattie on the grill. After it cooled, he placed it in McDuff's bowl while Susan prepared a plate of his favorite vegetable, raw cauliflower. After that, we all sat down to enjoy the meal.

Steven's parents finally gave in and got him a frisky German shepherd puppy named Lucky. All the plotting, planning, and weekend sleepovers paid off. Steven got his dog. Our plan succeeded. McDuff moved on to another student in the program, but with shocking results.

McDuff was assigned to a fifth grader named Maria, a sweet, dark-haired girl who told me on the first day how much she loved dogs. It's a pity the feeling wasn't mutual. McDuff simply refused to have anything to do with her.

He kept staring at the door while she read. I knew who he looked for. Every Saturday morning for twelve weeks, McDuff and Steven had spent time together in that reading room.

After about ten minutes into the session, McDuff jerked around and looked at me. *Where is Steven? What's this new kid doing sitting here?* She reached out and attempted to pat his head. He ducked away. At the end of the session, after being rebuffed many times, Maria turned to me and said, "I don't think he likes me."

"Oh, honey, he'll have to get used to you, that's all," I assured her with a sinking feeling.

That wasn't the truth. I never saw him react to anyone in that way since I owned him. He was friendly and outgoing to everybody, especially kids. The reason for his behavior didn't escape me. He expected Steven to read to him — no one else.

Immediately after the session, I reported to Florica what had taken place.

"He just misses Steven. Give him time. He'll come around," she said.

I had my doubts that he would warm up and accept his new reading partner. He didn't prove me wrong.

Oh sure, he sat there — like a black stone statue. Each time Maria attempted to pet him or show affection, he'd turn and look the other way. He didn't wag his tail, lick her face, or pay any attention to her at all while she read. Her only sin was not being Steven. I continued trying to assure her that he liked her. I could tell she didn't believe a word I said.

Thank goodness, the six weeks finally ended. It was torture sitting there and watching the disappointment in her eyes week after week. And, I worried it might affect her ability to improve her reading skills.

"Florica, I'm not going to start another session with McDuff and have another child feel rejected," I told her. She didn't try to change my mind.

The bond developed between Steven and McDuff in that reading room did not expand to include others. McDuff's refusal to accept his new Reading with Rover partner showed another side — a stubborn side — that frustrated the heck out of me.

# CHAPTER 12

# The Other Side

*We are impossibly conceited animals,*
*and actually dumb as heck. Ask any teacher.*
*You don't even have to ask a teacher. Ask anybody.*
*Dogs and cats are smarter than we are.*
*—KURT VONNEGUT, JR.*

DON'T THINK MCDUFF WAS SOME KIND OF FURRY ANGEL ALWAYS ON a mission. He had another side. His extreme intelligence combined with determination and stubbornness to create a humorous and frustrating little monster.

McDuff had a penchant for rolling in unsavory substances. Remember his obedience school graduation? Many times, I had to bring him home after our walks and give him a bath to wash out dog or cat poop matted in his thick, black fur. Anything dead he could find to roll on made his day.

I soon learned to look out when he stopped and dipped his right shoulder. I'd scream, "No roll!" and jerk hard holding him off the ground by his leash avoiding disaster; that is if I reacted fast enough. Getting him to take medication proved far more complicated.

Looking back, I see my naiveté the first time I attempted to give him a pill. Why should it be any different from medicating my other dogs? Just conceal it in something and give it to him. At least, that's what I thought before the first volley was fired at the beginning of the pill war.

Time after time, McDuff took from my hand the piece of wiener, lunch meat, or cheese with a pill tucked inside. He cautiously chewed once, then dropped it on the floor, and repeated the process until the pill popped out. After eating the food, he'd walk away smacking his mouth, leaving the tablet naked and exposed on the floor.

Frustrated, I told a friend at work about my problem. She suggested I put the pill far back in his throat and hold his mouth shut. Then, rub his throat until he swallowed it. She said that always worked with her dog. What she didn't know was my Scottie would come down with a bad case of lockjaw.

When I tried to open his mouth, he clinched his jaws tightly shut. He'd seen the pill hidden in my hand and knew what was going on. His staring straight into my eyes with a defiant glare made me laugh despite my attempt to control it. I broke down every time I tried to pry his clinched jaws apart. My friend had good intentions, but her suggestion didn't fly.

Another friend recommended putting the pill in peanut butter. "Does he like peanut butter?"

"I don't know, but he sure loves peanuts in the shell," I answered. So, I tried it.

He continuously smacked his mouth until the peanut butter melted, and then spat the pill out. To rub it in, he continued to smack and savor every trace of the peanut butter long after he strolled away. Foiled again.

In desperation, I called the veterinarian and told him about McDuff's antics. "Why don't you put it in some dog food?" he asked. *Why didn't I think of that?* I made a minor adjustment, because I fed him dry dog food, and canned better suited my purpose.

After checking the brands on the supermarket shelf, I bought the most expensive one I could find. For the price I paid compared to his dry food, I believe Wolfgang Puck was the pet food company chef.

With fiendish delight, I told McDuff about the delicious gourmet treat coming his way while the can opener hummed.

When he wasn't looking, I buried the pill in the middle of his dinner and casually strolled away. "Eat, Duff," I told him.

He sat there for what he believed to be a decent amount of time before he sauntered over to dine on the delicacy. Unlike my English Springer spaniel, Dawn, who I restrained with one leg while putting her food in the bowl, McDuff never, ever went to his food immediately. He wasn't about to give the appearance of being too eager. That wasn't dignified.

Sneaking back later, I checked and found the bowl licked clean, the pill nowhere in sight. *Outsmarted him at last!* After all, he was a dog dealing with a human. We are far superior to dogs on every level. All week I checked and found the bowl empty, and the pills gone.

McDuff ate his food in the laundry room. He had a dog bowl with a pet fountain container holding a gallon of water placed beside it. I noticed dirt and crud on the outside of his dog bowl, and decided it needed cleaning. Guess what I found when I lifted it up?

To my dismay, all the pills were neatly lined up in a row. He had hidden them in between the bowl and the water container, and not taken a single pill all week!

Worried and frantic with frustration, I telephoned his veterinarian again.

"McDuff hasn't taken his medication. I put the pills in his dog food like you told me to do. He ate the dog food and hid the pills. I've tried everything. What is there left to do?" I blurted out near hysterics and in tears. I knew he wouldn't get well without being medicated.

The doctor chuckled as I rambled on. "Calm yourself down," he soothed. "That McDuff is one smart dog. Come to the office, and I'll give you his medicine in capsule form. You can break them apart and mix the contents with his dog food."

I worried that McDuff would smell the medicine in his food and refuse to eat it. Thank goodness, he didn't. The pill battle ended. So, tell me something. Why did I feel I'd won the battle, but lost the war?

I had to come up with some way to appease my wounded pride and boost my confidence in dealing with that dog. I decided to teach him tricks. My previous dogs learned to sit up, lie down, roll over, and shake hands. Training them gave me pleasure, and they were eager to please.

It would be a piece of cake to teach a smart dog like McDuff a few simple tricks. Didn't he win the first place blue ribbon and trophy in his beginning obedience class? He performed perfectly at the TDI evaluation to become a certified therapy dog. Sure, he refused to carry the baton in his mouth at agility class, but he was older and more mature.

I chose to start with something easy like shaking hands, and move on to more difficult things. "Sit, Duff," I ordered, and he sat in the middle of the living room. Bending down, I lifted his foot while saying, "Shake," and repeated the procedure several times.

At first McDuff's foot was relaxed and soft when I lifted it, but it became more rigid as we progressed. Eventually, his foot was planted on the floor like a ten-ton concrete block. I had to force it up with both hands.

I knocked hard on the top of his toes with my knuckles to get him to lift his foot. That didn't work. He only pressed down harder. Kelly watched in amusement from the sofa. He offered to help me since he saw I wasn't making any progress.

Kelly and I worked for days with him and got nowhere. He simply refused to do it. There's no doubt in my mind McDuff understood what we wanted him to do. But, he declined to stoop to the level of other dogs and perform tricks. So much for that. I hadn't witnessed the ultimate demonstration of his stubbornness yet.

McDuff had been trained to use newspapers placed on the floor inside or go outside to do his business in the yard in Ohio. After I moved to the apartment in Nevada, I expected him to easily resume his dual training. He had different expectations.

Why should he go back to using newspapers inside? Everything was exciting and different in the desert — exotic smells to check out and unexplored territory to cover. He preferred to go outside, sniff around, and check out the new surroundings when he relieved himself. If Kelly or I didn't want to take him outside, he'd hold it. And, hold it, and hold it, and hold it. . . .

I fed him around eight a.m. and shut him in the laundry room with newspapers spread over the floor. It was his normal time to poop and pee on our morning walks, so I waited. After a while, I cracked open the door, peeped in, and saw nothing on the papers but McDuff's black butt. This went on for several hours. *Okay, if you want to play hard ball, I can do that*, I thought.

"Let's give him salty food and make him thirsty. I bet that will work," Kelly said.

Letting him out of the laundry room, we jam-packed him with pretzels, peanuts, and crackers. The only thing that came out of that bright idea was gas. Kelly and I fanned furiously with anything we could grab for relief from the overpowering stench. It smelled like rotten eggs. Hastily, I put him back in the laundry room. *It will be over soon. With fumes like that, he can't hold out much longer.*

It was eight p.m. by then, and still nothing on the newspapers. The skirmish had lasted all day. I started to weaken and think maybe it had gone on too long. "Maybe, I better take him outside," I said hoping Kelly would agree.

"McDuff's just being stubborn. We can wait him out," he replied shooting me a disapproving look. I wasn't so sure.

By eleven p.m., McDuff showed no signs of discomfort other than a worsening barrage of silent scorchers. He didn't exhibit signs of discomfort or indicate in any way that he wanted to go outside. Fearing the possibility of him suffering ill effects — and prosecution for animal abuse — I murmured, "Enough is enough! "

Avoiding my son's disapproving glower as we walked toward the door, I took McDuff outside. After almost causing me to fall in his hurry to get down the steps to the waiting grass, he must have peed for ten minutes without stopping.

Then, he hurried to do number two. Well, more like numbers two through six. But, what could you expect after fifteen hours of intense pressure? It's a wonder he hadn't exploded.

After a quick walk, we returned to face my son. Kelly sat with arms folded glaring at me when I came back inside with McDuff.

"Why did you cave in, Mom? McDuff's just stubborn. We could have waited him out."

I knew the Scottie reputation for stubbornness, and I knew my dog. He would have held it another fifteen hours, if necessary. Being hardheaded wasn't McDuff's only vice. He earned part of his AKC registered name because of something else.

He was a thief. Not a common thief, but the slickest four-legged one I've seen. He swiped things right out from under my nose. He once stole a pencil from me while sitting on my lap. The amazing thing is he did it without my seeing him do it.

When and how he managed to take it, I'll never know. I discovered it missing, and as I looked in the chair, he jumped down to the floor. Something happened that tripped him up, though. His different way of walking got him busted every time.

I've mentioned the unique Scottie walk before. McDuff's deviation from that walk got him nailed every time he stole something and attempted to get away. His movement changed to a slow, deliberate slink as he made his getaway. Whenever I saw it, I knew he had something in his mouth, even if I couldn't see his face.

"Drop it, Duff," I'd say sternly. And, out fell something of interest to him he didn't think I needed anymore, a pencil or pen, button, or candle. You name it. If it caught his fancy, he stole it. That's how he obtained the "Slick" in his AKC registered name, Debcha's Slick McDuff. My earlier research on the breed turned up something else, a connection to rodents.

One Halloween I bought him a large, black rubber rat with big ears and a long skinny tail. He went berserk when I gave it to him. Perhaps, it rekindled ancient memories of his ancestors hunting those pests in Scotland. I don't know, but he adored it.

Since it was made of hard rubber, he couldn't demolish it quickly the way he did his stuffed toys. It took him exactly one year. I know, because by the following Halloween, the poor thing was on its last leg, literally. Three of the legs were missing, the ears chewed off, and the tail missing. It was a pathetic sight.

I bought him a rat every Halloween because that is the only time I saw them in the stores. "Where's that rat?" I'd say when I wanted to mess with him. He'd race ahead of me, grab it, and dart away. No one touched his prized possession but him.

I must confess not being entirely truthful earlier when I said McDuff never destroyed anything in the house like other dogs. One Sunday afternoon, McDuff perched on the rug placed on top of the back of the sofa. It was his favorite place to look out of the picture window that took up most of the living room wall.

He watched for birds and other animals, especially squirrels. Cars and people going down the street caught his attention as well. I sat nearby in my high-back, easy chair with my feet propped up on the matching footstool watching the football game on television.

To this day, I don't know what McDuff spotted out of the window to excite him so much. Whatever he saw caused him to spring up and jut forward to get a better look. That's when he lost his balance and shot into the window head first.

The loud crack sounded like rifle fire and filled the room. Startled, I jerked my head in the direction of the noise to see what caused it. Nothing was on the back of the sofa. McDuff had disappeared.

I sprang up and stared at the shattered window with a hole in the middle of it. Alarmed, my eyes searched the driveway below looking for McDuff. That was silly of me, because the hole wasn't big enough for him to fall through. *He must be somewhere nearby, but where?* I thought.

"McDuff," I called his name and waited. Dead silence. *Did he knock himself unconscious when he struck the window? Is he lying somewhere bleeding to death?* I wondered. "McDuff!" I yelled, my voice rising in panic.

I heard a slight rustling from between the back of the sofa and the wall. I waited not knowing what to expect. Crawling out from under the lamp table that was between the end of the sofa and my chair, McDuff cowered down expecting me to holler at him. He had a *boy, I'm in for it now* expression on his downcast face.

"It's okay. I'm not mad at you," I whispered bending down to get a closer look at him.

Heck, I didn't care about the broken window. His being injured was my chief concern. I took his head into my hands being careful not to cause further injury, and searched for cuts, blood, or pieces of broken glass, maybe bones protruding through a fractured skull. To my relief, that repentant and scared Scottie didn't have a scratch on him. I lucked out on veterinarian bills that time.

The broken window was another matter. It had to be fixed, and because of its size, I anticipated paying big bucks. I called a glass repairman early Monday morning. After he inspected the shattered window, he turned to me and said, "Did someone shoot through your window?"

"Kind of," I answered. When I told him what happened, he looked at McDuff and couldn't stop laughing.

I'm glad he found it funny. When he told me the cost to repair it, I didn't see the humor. McDuff exhibited extreme caution on the back of the sofa after that. The window escapade was the only time he destroyed anything in the house. He differed from the average dog in another respect, too, in the unusual way he welcomed me home.

How does your dog greet you when you arrive home? Let me guess. I bet it's delirious with joy, barking, jumping up and down, and spinning in circles with delight. Right? Let me share how my dog welcomed me when I came home from work each day.

As soon as McDuff heard my key in the lock, he walked part way to the door. After he watched me come inside, he turned around, tail straight up in the air, and went directly to his toy basket on the floor in the hall.

"Hi, Duff. Come here, Boy," I'd say in my glad-to-see-you voice while beckoning him to come to me. Of course, that was before I learned the "routine."

He ignored me, intent on choosing the perfect toy from the basket. It took a few minutes as he nosed through them. Once he made his selection, my dog was ready to greet me. He'd walk up, drop his choice at my feet, and look at me. He expected me to throw the ball, tug on the rope, or whatever, until he got tired of playing.

Kelly rolled on the sofa with laughter as he watched the same scenario played out every day. To amuse him even more, I'd say in a hurt tone of voice, "Kelly, that's not the way other people's dogs greet them when they come home."

McDuff had a pet peeve that I mentioned earlier. He hated to have anything put on his body. To her dismay, my elderly neighbor witnessed just how much.

Darlene fell in love with McDuff on our walks around the neighborhood. Every morning she sat on her patio and waited for McDuff to come by and get his treat. It wasn't long before we became friends. We talked on the phone, went to lunch, and had each other over for dinner. My German-style sauerkraut and spareribs on New Year's Eve became an annual event.

Petite and neat, every strand of her white hair always in place, she was a kind, caring soul. Her attachment to McDuff grew with every passing day. He connected to something in her that only she and McDuff shared. She never grew tired of hearing about his therapy dog work and each new McDuff story.

I gave her a framed picture of him and a small pewter Scottie with a clock in it for Christmas. She promptly put his picture on top of her television among those of her grandchildren. That photo would become a source of comfort in her time of sorrow on a future Christmas. For now, she was happy, healthy, and full of excitement about something she planned to do for McDuff.

One day, she got the bright idea of making a hat and matching scarf for McDuff out of red, scotch-plaid material.

"Judy, he'll look so cute in them, and it will put a smile on the faces of the patients at the hospitals and nursing homes," she said sharing her vision with me.

I didn't have the heart to tell her to save her time and energy. No way would McDuff wear a hat — the scarf, maybe, but not the hat. Wearing a silly hat fell under the same category as doing tricks. And, we know he did not do tricks.

Darlene went about measuring his head and estimating how much material to purchase. Happily, she kept me informed of her progress, and soon the day for the dreaded first fitting arrived.

"Judy, bring McDuff over. His hat and scarf are ready. I can't wait to see him in them," Darlene said over the phone, anticipation tingling in her voice.

She stood in the middle of the living room floor when we arrived, hat and scarf in hand, with the biggest grin on her face.

"Come here, McDuff. Let Darlene put your hat on you."

McDuff dashed over to her. Glad to see her as usual, but ignoring the hat.

"Sit, McDuff," I commanded so she could arrange her creation. He obeyed without the slightest inkling of what was about to take place. She adjusted the hat until it rested on the right spot.

As soon as Darlene lifted her hands, McDuff ducked and shook his head like a buzz saw. The poor hat went skidding across the rug. Time after time, she adjusted the angle and tried to make it fit only to meet with the same results.

"I'll have to make some adjustments. Do you think tying it around his neck like a bonnet will help keep it on?" she asked with a frown.

"It might," I answered, not meeting her gaze. Sure, I know I should have warned her, but I didn't have the heart to shatter her hopes.

I dreaded the next fitting. Darlene had no intention of giving up. Neither did McDuff. By this time, he knew what to expect when he saw Darlene and the revolting hat. I had to order him to sit several times before he obeyed. Darlene placed it on his head, tied the band around his neck, and stood back.

First, McDuff tried the old duck-and-shake maneuver. It didn't work this time. Although now on the side of his head, the hat stayed put. He realized this called for extreme measures.

Pressing the side of his head and neck against the floor, with his hindquarters sticking up in the air, he churned his back feet and legs like propellers, all the while doing lazy S circles around the floor. The hat didn't stand a chance.

It ended up under the cocktail table, wrinkled and tossed aside like a used Kleenex. When I forced myself to look at Darlene, an expression of shock and disbelief, mixed with defeat, clouded her face.

"Hey, Darlene, I don't think the hat is going to work, but what about the scarf?" I asked, trying to divert her eyes from the demolished wreck she worked so hard to create.

She gave me a weak smile, nodded, and turned her attention to the scarf. Thank goodness, McDuff didn't protest wearing it. At least, she could derive some satisfaction from that.

Crushed, Darlene had to learn the hard way. If McDuff decided not to do something, you could cross it off your list. Maybe he disappointed her by not wearing the hat, but when she had something serious to deal with down the road, McDuff didn't let her down.

As you can see, McDuff wasn't a perfect angel or always that dignified creature on a mission. There's a fine line between an independent dog and a stubborn dog. McDuff did not know how to walk that line. But, he did know how to love unconditionally, another important lesson I learned from him during our time together.

CHAPTER 13

# Mcduff Loved Them All

*Love one another and you will be happy.*
*It's as simple and as difficult as that.*
—MICHAEL LEUNIG

WHAT BEGAN AS A PLEASANT DAILY MORNING WALK IN RODEO PARK turned into a nightmare. I noticed the man across the street from the park with two dogs, one a little frou-frou dog, and another medium-sized, long-haired mixed breed. A woman walked behind them with the largest pit bull I've ever seen.

The man's two dogs strained against their leashes to get to McDuff after they spotted him. He ignored them, too busy trying to get to those three bushes along the sidewalk that he sniffed forever and peed on every morning.

With growing uneasiness, I watched the man and his two dogs coming closer. Barking with increasing frenzy, their challenge rang out from the other side of the street to McDuff. As if watching in slow motion, I observed the monster pit bull begin to drag the protesting woman across the street toward us.

Her stocky body taut, leaning back, she pulled on the leash with all her might in an attempt to stop him, but to no avail. Closer and closer they came as I watched horrified. *Oh, no! She can't hold him back. He's going to attack McDuff!*

The man controlled his two dogs. It was another story for the woman. Although a large woman, she was no match for the pit bull's size and brute strength. She couldn't stop the

115

beast. His single focus was to get to McDuff, and nobody was going to stand in his way.

McDuff heard the panic registering in my voice and jerked his head around as I shouted, "Keep him over there. Stop him!"

She said nothing — just held on for dear life with reddening face and bulging eyes. That's when McDuff became aware of the snarling, slobbering menace lumbering his way like a slow-moving steamroller. I looked at my dog to gauge his reaction, praying he wasn't preparing to accept the challenge. I knew he didn't stand a chance and would certainly be killed if he fought the brute. Then, McDuff did the strangest thing.

Turning his back to the looming threat, he dropped down on his stomach, tucked his legs under him, and pulled his head into his chest on the ground. The pit bull pounced on him, and all hell broke loose.

I jumped away as it attacked McDuff with all the fury it could muster. The man had his hands full restraining his two dogs itching to get into the mêlée. The woman stood there with both hands on her cheeks, eyes wide, frozen in fright; the leash limp on the ground at her feet.

"Do something!" I screamed at her. "Get your dog off him!"

She didn't react, and it dawned on me. *She's terrified of him. She's not going to do anything. I've got to stop him from killing McDuff.*

Latched onto McDuff between the shoulders, the dog snarled and shook his massive head from side to side; spit flying as he bit into McDuff's back. *I've got to do something quick!* Without thinking or considering the consequences, I straddled the animal's back, put the fingers of both hands under his thick, wide collar, and yanked back as hard as I could.

"No! Stop it, stop it!" I screamed.

At first he ignored me, intent on inflicting all the punishment he could, but as I continued to tug and shout, he stopped. I can still see those golden eyes with tiny black dots for pupils, that flat, broad forehead, and pig-like ears as he turned his massive head and stared into my face. Saliva dripped from his mouth as he gave me a puzzled look.

I realized afterward he made the decision in that moment not to attack that crazy stranger riding his back. All the while the woman stood by watching, glued to the spot. I released my hold on the collar and slid off his back thinking it was finally over. I couldn't have been more wrong. He turned around and started mauling McDuff again.

Throughout it all, McDuff maintained the defensive posture he'd assumed pressed against the ground. He didn't move or attempt to defend himself in any way.

"Get over here and take these leashes!" the man roared at the panic-stricken woman. She snapped out of her stupor, ran and took hold of his two raging dogs. The man ran over to the mêlée, grabbed the leash lying on the ground, and tugged the protesting pit bull away.

My knees buckled, heart pounding in my chest as I watched the whole bunch of them hurry away, the two dogs still yapping and barking. The rogue pit bull rumbled away like an army tank with its mission to demolish the enemy accomplished.

"If you can't control that dog, you shouldn't take him out in public!" I yelled at their backs as they moved away, my voice quivering with fear and fury. No one inquired about the condition of my dog. They were in too big of a rush to get away to avoid assuming responsibility for the attack.

The man turned around, "I'm sorry," he apologized. The woman looked over her shoulder at me and said without missing a step, "You bitch."

*How am I the bitch when your dog attacked mine?* I wondered in amazement as I stared at their backs. McDuff lie motionless on the ground.

"McDuff," I said in a whisper. *Please, God, let him be alive.* I bent over and touched him with trembling hands.

At the touch of my hand, he sprang up and shook the way a dog does when it's had a bath. Not a glance in the direction of the gang scurrying away from us. I hesitated, too afraid to examine him for fear of encountering broken bones protruding through bloody skin. I ran my hands over his back. A wet, sticky substance covered them. *Oh, he's covered with blood.*

Examining my hands expecting to see them red and blood stained, I couldn't believe my eyes. No blood whatsoever, just a clear sticky substance. That couldn't be. Not after the brutal attack I'd just witnessed. *Where did the wetness come from?* It was saliva — his back drenched in it.

Thank goodness for that Scottish terrier double coat, and the loose skin on his back. Miraculously, McDuff suffered no injury whatsoever. Any other dog would be dead after such a terrible mauling. He knew what he was doing when he refused to fight, so unlike the typical combative Scottish terrier. And he knew enough to protect his head, throat, stomach, and legs. He knew how to take care of others; he could look out for himself, too.

McDuff never showed animosity toward the pit bull or any other dogs. He loved and accepted everybody and everything, except poor little Maria in the Reading with Rover program. Never once during our time together did I see him bare his teeth or growl in anger at any person or animal. Deviation from the pugnacious Scottie temperament saved his life that day in the park.

Pit bulls are known for aggressiveness, too. People fear and avoid them, but their bad reputation is undeserved in many cases. My cousin, Jimmy, has the sweetest pit bull in the world. He took Sam to obedience classes when he was a puppy. He and his wife, Paulette, continue to train and work with him.

The pit bull's awful reputation is largely due to irresponsible owners. The people we came into contact with in the park hadn't taken the time or made an effort to train and control their out-of-control menace, thereby creating a threat to others. The attitude of the woman and lack of concern for McDuff's welfare spoke volumes. Don't blame the pit bulls — blame their owners.

Unlike the typical Scottie, McDuff survived the attack by not fighting back. He was also different in another way, his fondness for cats.

McDuff loved cats, and couldn't figure out why the feeling wasn't mutual. To the dismay of cat owners waiting in the veterinarian's office, he refused to leave them alone. As he attempted to get close with his tail whipping in greeting, I'd pulled him away. The cats climbed up one side and down the other of their owners, spitting and clawing at him every inch of the way.

"I'm sorry. He only wants to play with them," I'd say with an apologetic smile. That didn't fix things. We both got cold stares. He looked up at me with a baffled expression as the cats hissed and batted at him with extended claws. *What's wrong with them? Why don't they ever want to play?* To his delight, he finally made one feline friend.

A young black cat with a white spot on its chest developed a unique relationship with McDuff. It made up for all the rejection he received from them elsewhere. Those two truly loved each other. I named the cat, Kitty Buddy.

"Look, Duff. There's your buddy," I'd say on our walks in the neighborhood.

He'd take off running on those squat legs toward her. Kitty Buddy waited for him to get near enough to rub against his chest, purring softy. With tail waving back and forth, McDuff's tongue caressed the top of her head.

No matter where they spotted each other, the greeting never varied. I've heard some dogs get along well with cats, but I've never owned one that did. McDuff enjoyed doing something else that most dogs hate. He loved visits to the veterinarian's office. To illustrate, let me tell about taking Scotty to the vet.

Scotty was a cocker spaniel and chow mix I got when Kelly was six years old. He had a nasty disposition and loathed trips to see the veterinarian. Because of his vicious temperament, chances to ride in the car and go places seldom happened. He instinctively knew when he got into the car where the journey would end.

Having to drag and stuff him into the car, and then tug him shivering and quaking from the parking lot into the waiting room irritated the heck out of me. Once inside, to my embarrassment, he snarled and growled at everything that moved or breathed.

Things didn't get any better in the examination room. Because of his vicious demeanor, I inherited the job of lifting him from the floor onto the stainless steel table. As soon as Scotty's feet left the floor, he started to urinate and didn't stop until plopped down in a yellow puddle. On our first visit, my clothes got soaked in front with warm dog pee. I learned after that to hold him out and away from my body while lifting him up. A visit to the veterinarian with him was a nerve-wracking experience for us. Taking McDuff was a joy.

McDuff went everywhere in the car with me and rode perched on the front edge of the passenger seat, looking out of the windshield or side window. He automatically shifted his weight and leaned when I rounded a curve, maintaining his balance.

The first time traffic conditions called for an abrupt stop, he flew head first off the seat like a guided missile, landing in the small space in front of the seat with a thud. With difficulty, he maneuvered his chunky body around in the limited space to face me.

*Why in the world did you do that?*

"I'm sorry, Duff," I said, trying not to laugh. "I couldn't help it."

From then on, every time I foresaw a slam-on-the-brakes situation, I'd say, "Down, Duff." He collapsed down on all fours and hung on. After coming to a stop, I'd say, "Okay." He'd push up and assume his position roosting on the edge of the seat like a canary. Curious motorists driving alongside pointed and stared at us.

Unlike Scotty, a ride in the car didn't indicate a trip to the veterinarian's office to McDuff. It wouldn't have mattered, anyway. It was a favorite destination for him. Nice people with treats, other dogs, and best of all, cats, waited there.

I decided to board him at his doctor's office while taking a vacation one year, and wondered if he'd change his opinion. Boarding in a cage for a week as opposed to an office visit were two different things. I found out after hurrying like crazy to get back from my trip to pick him up.

*I hope I make it there in time!* I thought, checking my watch for the fiftieth time as I drove faster. The receptionist told me when I called earlier the office closed at six p.m., but they would wait until around seven for me to get there.

I'd missed McDuff, and desperately wanted to get back in time to pick him up. I knew how social he was, and it bothered me thinking of him being caged up for days. *He must be going crazy and wondering why he's been abandoned,* I thought, my guilty conscious kicking in big time.

I rolled into the parking lot a few minutes before seven. "I made it!" I shouted in joy. The receptionist looked up and smiled as I rushed through the door.

"We wondered if you were going to get back in time. Everyone's getting ready to leave," she said.

"I had my doubts. Where's my McDuff?" I replied, beaming ear to ear.

"I'll get him for you," she said and left the room.

It didn't take long to hear sharp nails clicking against the tile floor, growing louder at a swift pace. McDuff blasted into the room.

"Hi, Duff. Come here, boy. I missed you!" I said, grabbing for him. He rushed up, gave a quick lick, turned a quick circle around me, and dashed out of the room. The receptionist couldn't miss the stunned look on my face. A white-coated doctor with a stethoscope around his neck emerged from the back.

"Mrs. McFadden, I have to tell you all of us here love McDuff. He's a character. We let him out every night to make rounds with us. Oh, by the way. We upgraded him to a run and got him out of that cage. I hope he didn't gain weight from the treats. We're sure going to miss him around here."

I felt like a bride left at the altar — humiliated and rejected.

"Yep, everyone loves McDuff," I said with a feeble smile on my lips.

He had the time of his life on his vacation with the doctors. Although McDuff fit in well with humans, he made himself equally at home with ducks.

McDuff felt an attraction to ducks. Once, while Kelly and I walked him in Franklin Park, he jumped into a pond to get near a gaggle of wild ducks. As we approached, they spooked. Quacking in panic, ducks scattered and entered the pond from all directions trying to get away from him. He took it as an invitation to join them for a swim.

Before I could stop him, he took a running leap from the bank, jumped about four feet in the air, and landed in the water like a stone.

He stayed under so long I prepared to dive in to rescue him. The fact I can't swim didn't factor in at all. Probably would have done mouth-to-mouth resuscitation on him, if necessary. To make matters worse, the pond didn't contain fresh water. Stagnant, pea-green scum floated on top around the bank.

After what seemed like ages, he bobbed to the top, dog paddled in a circle until he spotted the ducks, and took off like a torpedo to catch up with the flock.

"McDuff, NO! Come back here!"

He turned around in the water, spotted me on the bank, and took his sweet time swimming back. Let me tell you, riding home in a car with a stinking, wet, slime-covered dog is not my idea of a walk in the park. But, the encounter between McDuff and a frightened, lost baby duck during a move to a new apartment proved to be the most bizarre of all.

Moving to me is like having a tooth pulled. It's the last thing in the world I want to do. When it's because of someone else, that makes it worse. I'd started to see cockroaches in my kitchen, and it enraged me. Out of the door I stormed to the rental office.

"There are roaches running around in my kitchen. I've lived here two years and nothing like that has happened before. Let me tell you something. I refuse to live anywhere with bugs," I yelled at the startled manager.

"Judy, please calm down. We'll get to the bottom of this. You got new neighbors on the other side of your apartment, and that's probably where the roaches came from. Other tenants have complained, too. We'll spray and that will take care of it."

"No way, I'm not dealing with spraying and harmful chemicals over everything. I'm out of here."

"You're one of our best tenants. We don't want you to move away. Would you reconsider if we moved you into a larger apartment with a fireplace?

"Well . . . let me think about it. I'll let you know." Sure, I was outraged about the roaches, but it didn't cloud my senses. Recognizing a good offer when I heard one, I accepted and started packing to move to a nicer place.

One evening while taking moving boxes from the car, the weirdest noise pierced the air. Something was in terrible distress, but what? It sounded like a bird of some kind. I knew one thing for sure. If the racket kept going, one of the neighborhood cats would soon come to check it out. With box in hand, I followed the sound. That's when I spotted it — a tiny wild duckling shrieking at the top of its lungs.

The wind storm that day must have blown it from the Henderson Bird Preserve where all species of birds and ducks resided. I once saw a blown-off-course pelican there after a similar storm. This little orphan was lost, alone, and terrified. All I had to do was catch him and take him back. That shouldn't pose a problem. But, I found out why they're called ducks.

I grabbed a box and started chasing it. He ducked under everything he could to get away from me. Like greased lightning, he zigzagged across the ground with me in hot pursuit, the ruckus alarming the entire neighborhood. Finally, I got near enough to drop the box over him. Trapped at last! I waited for the fluttering and scrambling to cease.

Reaching cautiously under the box, my hand clamped over the soft body, I picked him up. Tiny featherless wings beat up and down, legs churned and clawed. He struck out at me with his hard bill. He wasn't going down without a fight.

For a moment, I thought about turning him loose. Then, I remembered the cats. He wouldn't stand a chance. Like it or not, we were stuck with each other.

As I entered the apartment with this little demon wailing like something from the underworld, McDuff came thundering down the hall. Up on his hind legs, with front legs flailing, he tried to get a closer look at what was struggling in my hands.

"Down, Duff! Get back!" I ordered, holding the fighting duckling high over my head. I remembered my English Springer spaniel, Dawn, accidentally killed an orphaned baby rabbit I brought home once. *I'll have to keep McDuff far away from him.*

Exhausted, I sat down on the living room sofa holding the struggling duckling out in front of me with both hands. *When is this thing going to calm down?* That's when another eerie incident with McDuff took place.

He approached us at a slow, deliberate pace, body low to the floor. I saw the familiar "stare." He fixed his eyes on the frightened creature while creeping closer and closer, stopped and reached out and touched its bill with the tip of his nose. Spellbound, as though in a trance, it ceased to move or make a peep, becoming deadly still. They stayed that way as I watched, mesmerized.

It seemed like a long time, but probably after a minute or so, McDuff broke away, backed up, and looked at me. I sat there transfixed. I'd seen the mystical look before and its effect on people. Now, I witnessed this supernatural ability applied to a panic-stricken creature in need of comfort. It also became clear to me that McDuff's uncanny ability to connect extended beyond humans.

Putting the tranquil duckling back in the box, I reached for the phone and called the bird preserve. To my dismay, a recorded message notified me it was after hours and to call back in the morning. *Just my luck. What am I going to do with it until tomorrow? What can I feed it? Where will I put it tonight?* Thoughts zoomed through my mind.

McDuff curiously watched my every move and followed me to the kitchen. My mom fed bread to the birds in her yard, maybe ducks liked it, too. I got a piece, broke it into small pieces, and dropped them in the box. My unappreciative guest paid no attention to the bread and began a mad scramble and suicidal bouncing against the sides of the box.

Since I struck out on the food, I pondered where he'd spend the night. The box seemed cold and impersonal. *I got it! Ducks like water, so I'll put him in the bathtub.* Running down the hall to the bathroom, I filled the tub with enough water for swimming and placed a bath towel at the sloping end to permit him to get out of the water. *Now, the problem remains what to feed him.*

I'd been so preoccupied I forgot to eat dinner. When I went into the kitchen and turned on the light, a roach on the counter by the sink froze like an icicle in the arctic and then scurried out of sight. *That's it! Birds and ducks eat insects, preferably alive. I'll catch roaches and give them to him.* I knew my plan would work.

Smiling in fiendish delight, I turned off the light. With a paper towel in my hand, I stood and waited a few minutes in the dark. On snapped the light and a juicy roach made a mad dash for cover. Too late; the unlucky intruder got trapped. Off to the bathroom I raced with my prize.

I dropped the squirming bug out of the paper tower into the water, and watched it swim around in circles. Like scissors cutting through silk, the duckling swam after it. Chug-a-lug. One roach down, and approximately ten more to go before the empty stomach failed to show interest in the sacrificial offerings. Later that night, I crept into the bathroom. My visitor, belly full of bugs, slept peacefully on the fluffy, white towel.

Early the next morning, with noisy objection coming from the box on the back seat, I set off to the bird preserve. A mother duck with six small ducklings made room for one more without the least bit of hesitation. The family paddled away making ripples across the pond while I watched with a grateful heart. I reflected on what I'd learned from this duck experience.

All creatures on earth have a purpose, even the lowly cockroach. The insects I ranted and raved against became the source of sustenance for a lost, scared out-of-his-wits duckling and led to a better apartment for me. And, it confirmed McDuff's uncanny effect to communicate and comfort. But, he wasn't always on his mission. McDuff was a party animal. He knew how to have fun.

He loved the holidays and get-togethers. Christmas meant a visit with Jennie. My friend, Linda, who had gone with me to pick up McDuff, returned to the same Ohio kennel a few months later and got a female wheaten-colored Scottish terrier. McDuff and Jennie became good buddies. They visited and exchanged Christmas presents every year. Jennie was the only dog that matched McDuff in level of energy and intensity. It must be a terrier thing.

I had no idea that McDuff was a party animal until he received an invitation to my office Christmas party. At first I thought it was a joke.

"I'm serious. Please bring McDuff to the party, Judy. Everyone has heard so much about him and wants to meet him," my boss reiterated before leaving the office on Friday.

Against my better judgment, I took him with me to my boss' upscale home in Dublin, Ohio that cold December, Saturday evening. His water rationed that afternoon to prevent any "accidents," I made sure he had relieved himself before we drove off to the party.

The first thing I noticed when we entered the splendid home was the oriental rugs on the floor. *McDuff doesn't have to pee or poop, so don't worry about it*, I thought, trying to quell my nerves. All attention centered on him when we entered the door. I let him off his leash, but kept him close to me to keep an eye on him.

As the merrymaking progressed, McDuff began to circulate. Suddenly, I realized he was no where in sight. I'd gotten caught up in a conversation with a co-worker, and he slipped away. "Where's McDuff?" I asked anxiously noticing his absence from the room. "Oh, don't worry, Judy. He's with me," the lady of the house replied from the kitchen. "He's so cute."

Ignoring the nagging voice in my head saying, *are you sure he's not going to make some kind of a mess?* I didn't call him back into the room with me. Although, from time to time, I went to the kitchen to check on him. He was having a ball, the center of attention, and eating hors d'oeuvres. Then it happened.

A voice from the kitchen said, "Judy, McDuff was so thirsty that he drank three bowls of water, and guess what?" *I knew it! I knew it! You shouldn't have let him out of your sight,* the little voice in my head screeched.

A vision of pee stains soaking through the rich tapestry onto the floor below danced through my head. Or worse yet, steaming tan dog turds stacked up in a neat pile. Little needles of humiliation pricked my skin from head to toe, and with a dry mouth, I squeaked, "What did he do?"

"He followed someone outside onto the deck, went down the steps into the backyard and peed. After that, he came back inside on his own. He's just too much."

Waves of relief swept over me. And, another feeling with it — shame for lack of faith in my dog. I knew better than anyone he wasn't an ordinary dog. He didn't need supervision; he knew what to do. I relaxed and enjoyed the evening after that. Party animal, McDuff, had fun, too. Christmas wasn't his favorite holiday though. Halloween filled him with excitement every year with the steady stream of costumed characters.

Halloween meant more than a new rubber rat to McDuff. It meant trick-or-treaters with containers filled with candy. He'd wait for the doorbell to ring and race to get me if I was out of the room. While I handed out candy, he poked his head out of the door for pats. But, an innocent little angel came face to face with the "Slick" side of McDuff one evening.

As I doled out candy to a motley crew of costumed kids on the porch, a loud wail arose. "No, stop it!" A torrent of tears streamed down the face of the pint-sized angel with a crooked halo. Dressed in white with sheer wings shimmering in the breeze, she couldn't have been more than four years old, and cute as can be.

Her mother stumbled in her haste trying to get onto the porch, a frown of concern on her face. I looked down at the little girl and immediately detected the problem. McDuff's head was buried in the little girl's pumpkin container gobbling up the candy inside. "Drop it, Duff. Get out of there!" I commanded, jerking his head out of the orange pail.

After reassuring the worried mother her little angel had not been bitten by the bad dog, I turned to see Slick slinking away with a mouthful of goodies. That was his first and last raid on a trick-or-treater. I watched him carefully after that night. McDuff loved crowds, but he excelled in one-on-one connections as well.

He and my good friend, Trudy, formed a special bond. She had told me about the kennel where I got him. Trudy had two Lhasa Apsos she was crazy about.

"I love Jasmine and Bandit, Judy, but they're not like McDuff. McDuff is special," she'd tell me.

She howled with laughter at the McDuff stories, as did my other friends at Vorys. He was included on our Christmas visits to her house, much to the annoyance of Jasmine and Bandit. Hyperactive terriers and sophisticated Lhasa Apsos don't mix.

Trudy and Dolores were my first visitors when I moved to Nevada. After returning back to Ohio, Trudy called and told me a secret she and McDuff shared during her visit.

It seems that one morning around six a.m., nine a.m. Ohio time, she opened her bedroom door to go to the bathroom. There sat McDuff facing the door waiting for her to open it and come out. When she went back into the bedroom, McDuff slipped in with her. She got in bed only to have McDuff jump up and join her.

They napped until she heard someone stirring around. Springing out of bed, she shoved McDuff out, and shut the door. They went through that routine every day of her stay. I believe McDuff sensed it would be the last time we would see Trudy alive.

My dear friend died from leukemia at the age of fifty-three. We talked on the phone or e-mailed almost every day, growing even closer after I moved from Ohio to Nevada. I knew how hard she fought the cancer. When it came back for the third time, our conversations turned to death and how we viewed it.

She told me she was ready to see her mother who had died a few years before. After a long and courageous battle, including a bone marrow transplant, Trudy went to be with her mom. I still miss her to this day.

I learned a great many lessons from McDuff while observing his interaction with my friends and other animals. When the pit bulls of life attack, take a non-resistant attitude, cover yourself with prayer and faith, and when it's over, walk away without looking back. Love those cats who are supposed to be your enemies. Enjoy the holidays and be a fun-loving, party animal. Comfort those who are frightened, lost, or facing the valley of death when they pass through your life.

My teacher, travel companion, and guide wouldn't always be with me. I didn't know it, but McDuff's mission was winding down.

# CHAPTER 14

# Beginning of the End

*It is not length of life, but depth of life.*
—RALPH WALDO EMERSON

**M**cDUFF SAT ON THE FLOOR LICKING HIS LEFT HIND FOOT. AT FIRST, I thought nothing of it. Allergies sometimes caused him to lick his feet before we left Ohio. When it increased, I examined his foot, and found nothing out of the ordinary.

A few weeks later he began to limp. I took another look. That's when I detected a small, soft bump on the side of his foot that caused him to jerk away when I touched it. *Probably nothing serious, but I'll take him to the vet and have it checked out,* I thought.

I wasn't overly concerned when I drove to the veterinarian's office that morning. After they examined him and took X-rays, I didn't receive a satisfactory explanation of what caused the problem, only possibilities, nothing definitive.

The doctor wrapped McDuff's foot, and scheduled another appointment for a progress check. This went on several more weeks without any improvement. Too much time had passed. Something wasn't right, and I wanted to get to the bottom of it. I knew I'd have to go somewhere else to get an answer.

"His foot is not getting any better, and I'm not satisfied with his treatment here. I'll take him to another veterinarian for a second opinion. If there's agreement with your treatment, I'll bring him back," I said after our visit.

I'd learned about the value of second opinions when I worked as a counselor on the National Cancer Institute phone line. Why should it be any different for animals? Of course, all the trips to the different doctor's offices would make McDuff happy. He loved contact with people, other pets, and the treats.

Leaving the office, I drove directly to another veterinarian located in the same part of town. Before he would examine McDuff, he wanted to see his X-rays. I went back to the original veterinarian's office and got them. The new doctor examined McDuff's foot, looked at the X-rays, and told me, "There's a possibility the lump might be cancerous. I'll do a biopsy."

*Cancer!* The word hit me in the stomach like a hammer. I'd been trying not to think of that possibility, although it lingered in the back of my mind. I remembered reading that Scotties were prone to skin cancer, particularly melanoma.

*Was moving out here to the desert and walking him in the heat and sunlight with his black coat detrimental? His toenails and even the soles of his feet are black. Could that be a risk factor?* My mind raced from one thought to another. I'd have to wait for the results of the biopsy to find out.

Back home, I watched McDuff's tongue caressing his now unbandaged foot in an attempt to sooth the pain. I anxiously waited, and at the same time, dreaded the biopsy results. Time crawled by, and after a few days, I received a phone call requesting me to come to the office.

"Mrs. McFadden, I have bad news and good news for you. The bad news is that the lump is cancerous. The good news is, because it's located on the side of his foot, it can be removed easily. However, a part of his foot will have to be amputated with it."

Fear gripped my heart like a vise. Although I tried to prepare myself for the worst, the diagnosis shocked me. And, something else bothered me. *Did the cancer have time to spread?*

We scheduled a date for the surgery, and I left the office. The stoic front I displayed in the office crumbled after I got into the car. I cried all the way home. McDuff knew something troubled me. He touched my hand on the steering wheel with his cold nose and watched me with his searching dark eyes. I patted his head and that seemed to relax him.

I realized a lot of time had elapsed from his first symptom and the date of cancer diagnosis. That couldn't be good. No matter what, I'd try to make it easy as possible for him. The thought of putting him through the pain of surgery distressed me. How I wished there was another way.

The morning of the surgery arrived. McDuff looked for his food and water. The doctor said nothing to eat or drink before surgery. I knew he was hungry and puzzled. My nerves jangled as we got into the car. The closer we got to the office, the tenser I became. I could tell by the way McDuff kept glancing over at me as I drove that he knew something was up.

As usual, the office staff made a big fuss over him when we arrived. We sat down by a lady holding a playful puppy in her lap. She looked back and forth several times at McDuff and me. "Is his name McDuff? Was he on television?"

"Yep. That's him," I said as I took him in to see the doctor. This time, McDuff stayed behind when I left.

After the surgery, and a few days' stay to recuperate, I went to pick him up. When I entered the room, I spotted the hard, white covering on his lower leg and what remained of his foot. A shaved spot on his side contained a pain patch, and a lampshade-like device around his neck prevented him from removing the wrapping.

His eyes locked on mine. *What's happening? Why did you let them do this to me? I don't like it one bit.*

I reassured myself I'd done the right thing. But, at the back of my mind, the same thought nagged at me. *Did the cancer have time to spread?*

Although uncomfortable, McDuff came through like a champ. Scotties are known for being tough and courageous. Whining and flinching from pain aren't options. It's bred into them. Before long, the bandage, pain patch, and neck device were removed.

To my relief, having part of his foot missing didn't hamper him at all — not even a slight limp. That Scottie strut remained intact. Life returned to "happily ever after," like in the fairy tales. There's just one thing. We all know life is not a fairy tale.

Denial is strange. Even while in the midst of it, you are aware of what you are trying to deny. I convinced myself the limp I noticed came from tenderness in McDuff's foot because of the surgery six months before. He began licking it again, but I told myself it didn't mean anything, probably just a tingling. I knew though — deep inside, I knew.

When I forced myself to examine his foot, I felt a small lump growing out of the same area where the amputation occurred. Once again he yanked back when I touched it. The next day I made an appointment and took him in.

The fairy tale turned back into reality. The cancer had returned. I listened as the doctor suggested the course of treatment with my mind in a haze.

"I recommend amputation of the leg followed by chemo-therapy," he said.

"Can you assure me the cancer hasn't spread to other areas?"

"No, I can't do that."

"Then, I'll think it over and get back to you with my decision."

Why put McDuff through amputation and pain more severe than his previous surgery without assurance that the cancer hadn't spread elsewhere? He was nine-years-old. Sure, surgery might allow me to keep him a few years longer, but at what price to him?

I saw the way he looked at me when I went to pick him up that day. He wasn't pleased by what he'd been through. I called the doctor's office the next morning.

"Amputation is out of the question. With the possibility that the cancer may have metastasized, I'm not putting him through it again. No thanks."

We agreed to keep him on pain pills and monitor his progress. At first, the pills kept the pain in check. He ate everything put in front of him and seemed fine. But, I knew he would withstand pain without displaying discomfort. Other than cutting back on the distance of our walks, everything else remained the same.

My friends in Ohio, members of Unity in Green Valley, a trans-denominational spiritual center I attended in Henderson, and Unity Village Development Department in Missouri knew about McDuff's cancer. They proved to be a source of great comfort and support to me.

Kitty, my friend at the Development Department, told me they prayed for McDuff three times a day. I prayed too, but not for a specific outcome as before. This time, I placed him in God's hands. I knew there was something mystical about McDuff and his mission on earth. Perhaps, it was coming to an end, and time for him to move on.

It broke my heart to think of losing him. On the other hand, I recognized how blessed and fortunate I was to have a special creature like him in my life. Time would reveal the will of God for McDuff. I set about savoring whatever time we had left.

I was invited to speak at the Sunday devotional service about McDuff and volunteering with TDI. He knew we were going to do therapy dog work when I put the red leash on him that morning. I also put on his bright red therapy dog vest. I knew the members would be surprised to see him there. However, not everyone welcomed a dog in church that morning.

A mother with the cutest little girl in a blue flowered dress with matching ornament in her curly dark hair came into the room. She looked to be about three- or four-years-old. As soon as she spied McDuff, she screamed, "No, Mommy! Doggie, Doggie! " climbing and clawing her mother's legs in an attempt to escape into her arms.

The mother looked at McDuff in astonishment as she attempted to calm her hysterical, crying child. It became obvious at least one member wasn't aware of the theme for Sunday's service. How often do you see a dog in church?

"Stay, Duff," I said rushing over to the pair. "I'm sorry he scared her. He's really friendly, but I'll make sure he stays away from your little girl."

The child's arms wrapped around her mother's neck and her tiny face pressed tightly against her mother's chest as she whimpered softly.

"She was frightened by a large dog and has been terrified like this ever since," the mother explained.

When it was time for my talk, we walked to the front of the church. I commanded McDuff to lie down and began to speak. I told the members about TDI and requirements to become a therapy dog, the places we visited, his work with the disabled residents at Project PRIDE, Steven and the Reading with Rover Program, and the little girl in the emergency room at St. Rose Dominican Hospital.

Eyes misted as I talked about McDuff's cancer surgery. I told them of the prayer circles across the country and at Unity Village. Then, I informed them that the cancer had reoccurred.

Tissues dabbed at tear-stained eyes. The sound of discreet nose blowing reverberated throughout the sanctuary. I began to choke up, but willed myself not to give in to my emotions. I ended by saying, "Now, I have placed McDuff in God's hands. His will be done, and His will may be that soon McDuff's mission will be finished on this plane. I've seen the joy he has brought to others. I know the joy he has brought me far outweighs the pain I will feel at losing him."

The whole congregation wept. The few men who'd been trying to hang tough joined the women. Kathryn, a slender woman with sparkling, expressive eyes and brown, gold-streaked hair approached McDuff. She bent over, and with her tears falling like rain onto his head, tied a blue ribbon with a small gold bone hanging from it around his neck. On it was engraved, *To McDuff, For Loving Service. Our Hero.*

It took her a while to regain composure enough to resume. After the service ended, while receiving comforting hugs, I overheard a man say to another man, "I was doing okay until my wife broke down. Then, I lost it, too."

Having the support, sympathy, and understanding of so many people uplifted me. The prospect of putting a faithful companion down is agonizing. It made a difference knowing I didn't have to face the heartbreak alone.

It's hard for some people to understand the love and devotion one can feel for pets, and how pets touch our lives. "They're only animals," they say with disdain. But, that's so untrue. They may be animals, but they are more than that.

They are unconditional love on four legs, anchors in a storm when we are tossed around by the waves of life, the answer to the lonely and abandoned in an uncaring world, therapy for the sick and impaired, and a source of joy that uplifts spirits with a lick of the tongue. They sometimes do for us what those closest to us can't or won't do.

People who say they are only animals have not walked into a nursing home with a therapy dog and seen an elderly resident, who never received visitors and refused to communicate, light up and come to life. Or, a person lying in a hospital bed wracked with pain and fear reach out to pet a furry head, smiling and forgetting their suffering for a while. Or, individuals who can't see, talk, or walk, and are in diapers, smile in response to a gentle warm tongue on their faces.

Those persons who believe pets shouldn't be treated like our children haven't experienced the depth of despair caused by an acrimonious divorce, tragic death of a parent, and loss of employment all hitting like sharp darts thrown one after another. And throughout it all, receiving strength and comfort from an animal companion who's with you every step of the way.

Believe me, if they had encountered any of those things the way I did, never again would they say, "They're only animals."

I circulated among the congregation while McDuff roamed around off leash. After a while, immersed in conversation and enjoying the refreshments, I lost track of him. When I looked around to check on his whereabouts, he was socializing, too. It didn't concern me. He wouldn't cause any problems, and the traumatized child stuck close to her mother, eyeing McDuff warily from a distance.

When it happened is still a mystery to me. One minute the little girl was by her mother's side, the next minute having a private tea party with McDuff at the refreshment table. She ate a cracker and gave a cracker to McDuff. She ate a piece of cheese and gave a piece of cheese to McDuff. She ate a cookie and gave a cookie to McDuff.

I waved my hand in the air to get the mother's attention and pointed to them from across the room. Her mother looked in that direction and exclaimed, "I can't believe what I'm seeing. She is terrified of dogs."

As we walked over to them, shock registering on her mother's face, the little girl looked up at us and said with a big grin, "McDuff likes cheese and crackers."

"I think McDuff's had enough to eat, Baby. It's time for us to leave now," her mother said, taking her hand and leading her away.

As they left the church, the little girl stopped before going out the door, turned and shouted loud enough for everyone to hear, "Good-bye, McDuff," — and blew him a big kiss.

All of the sadness in the room dissolved like snow melting in the warm rays of the sun. Once again, he worked his spirit dog magic. A fear firmly entrenched in a child's mind evaporated in a single morning because of him.

McDuff's mission touched and changed the lives of so many, from the very young to the very old. But, how much longer did he have to complete that mission?

# CHAPTER 15

# Never Again

*Grief is so painfully real, regardless of its origin.*
*The love of, and attachment to, an animal friend*
*can equal that of human relationships. Likewise,*
*the loss of an animal can be just as devastating.*
— REV. JOEL L. MORGAN

**M**cDUFF SPENT MUCH OF HIS TIME ATTENDING TO HIS ACHING FOOT. I knew the pain pills weren't working. The dosage had been increased from one pill to a pill and a half. When that didn't afford relief, I gave him two.

A slight improvement occurred after that, but it didn't last long. He wasn't up to his old tricks about taking medication either, a sign of how terribly wrong things were with him.

The pain kept him awake at night. Since he slept in my bedroom, that meant I didn't sleep either. His suffering became my suffering. Do you know how it feels to stand by and watch helplessly while someone or something you love suffers? I'd experienced it with my mother and now with McDuff.

I had done all I could do to offer relief, but nothing helped. I started experiencing what he endured. If he didn't sleep, I didn't sleep; if he didn't eat, I lost my appetite. I think, in my mind, it made me feel that I was assisting him in some small way.

I hated going to work and leaving him alone. He didn't outwardly indicate what I knew he was going through. That was McDuff for you, stoic and brave, displaying his inbred courage and dignity. He didn't whimper, whine, or show any signs of irritability or discomfort. That just wasn't his style. I couldn't let him suffer indefinitely. Yet, something prevented me from making the decision to put him down.

I awakened in the wee hours one morning and heard McDuff on the floor at the bottom of my bed. For years, he had slept on the bed with me, but stopped after the surgery. I think the weight of his body put too much pressure on his healing foot when he jumped down.

Slipping from under the covers and onto the floor, I went down on my hands and knees. At eye level, I looked at him sitting in front of me waiting for me to speak.

"Duff, this isn't working. Things don't look so good. The pain pills aren't doing any good. It's killing me to see you suffer like this. I think it's time."

He licked his foot, raised his head, and gazed deep into my eyes. We stayed locked together that way for a while. Then, he lowered his head, and his tongue caressed the back of my hand one time. Looking up, he stared deeply into my eyes again — the last time I saw that wise and mystical "stare." *It's alright with me. Do what you have to do.*

McDuff had made the decision for me that I found so hard to make. Somehow, I had to find the strength to carry it out. I called work early the next morning and spoke to my supervisor.

"I'm taking off today. It's time to put McDuff out of his pain." Then, I hung up and called the veterinarian's office.

"Tell McDuff's doctor I'm bringing him in this morning. The pills he prescribed aren't relieving the pain, even though I've doubled the dosage. It's time to put him down."

As we stepped onto the porch, I looked at the rough, hard surface of the steps outside my apartment. I knew they would intensify his suffering. We started to descend the eighteen stone steps. My mind drifted back to the first time he confronted them years ago. The way he refused to go up or down for so long. Maybe he knew how they'd add to the misery of his last hours on earth.

I thought about carrying him down, but dismissed that idea right away. He hated to be picked up and carried. I knew he'd feel undignified being carted around like other dogs. Unlike going limp the way he did when he was a puppy, he became stiff and uncomfortable. Respect for his obstinate pride stayed with me to the end.

Agony must have throbbed through his body with every step. He stopped midway down, panting heavily before slowly continuing to the bottom. He struggled to cover the short distance to the garage, pausing twice to sit and rest. I could tell the hurt from tackling the stairs had taken a lot out of him.

He needed help getting into the car, and flopped down on his side with a sigh. As we drove off, it dawned on me. Never again would I look over and see him perched like a bird on the passenger seat on our rides. That's when the impact of what was going to take place hit me like a sledgehammer.

Upon arrival at the office, he perked up a bit, but the old days of bothering the cats and other animals were over. Lying exhausted on the floor by my feet, he hardly noticed them. After a short wait, we were ushered into the treatment room.

I went through the open door. The shiny metal table stood out, menacing and overshadowing everything in the room. The doctor cut short his attempt to put me at ease. He knew I wasn't listening to a word he said. He lifted McDuff gently onto the table and explained the procedure to me.

I held him in my arms for the last time while the doctor administered the shot. Those eyes I loved and learned so much from brightened and bore into mine before the injection took effect. I watched their radiance ebb, become dull, listless, and fade away as life slithered out of his body.

Those of you who have been down this road know how unbelievably fast the shot works. Within a matter of seconds my teacher and companion was gone. I released the lifeless vehicle from my arms that had once contained McDuff. Laying him down on the sterile cold table, I forced my weak, trembling legs to walk out of the room. I left his body behind, but I carried his spirit away in my heart forever on that sad day.

"Do you want to make arrangements for cremation or burial?" the lady asked as I rushed by the front desk without stopping. I shook my head, blinded by tears, and stumbled out of the door to my car parked out front.

Many pet lovers tell of the special places of burial for the remains of a beloved pet. Under a tree in the backyard, or scattered to the wind in a favorite park. Or, perhaps they placed the remains in an urn to be displayed at a place of honor in their homes. Not me. Not for McDuff.

I realized early on that he didn't belong to me. I had shared him with others his whole life. He wanted it that way. Because he hadn't been confined to me in life, I couldn't selfishly claim him in death. His mission was to comfort and bring joy to others, and he never once deviated from that duty. I accompanied him on his journey, but he wasn't mine.

I broke down in the car, unable to drive away. It was twenty minutes before I pulled myself together enough to start the engine. The office staff curiously peeped out of the window from time to time. No one came outside to console me, or offer support.

It didn't matter. Nothing or nobody on the face of the earth could have comforted me after losing McDuff on that Halloween morning. He wouldn't be there with me to greet the trick-or-treaters ever again.

Flinging my body on the living room sofa as soon as I got home, loud, wracking sobs penetrated the silence. I wept all day Saturday, and when I attended church on Sunday morning, I sat apart from the congregation with quiet tears flowing in streams.

Without asking, the members knew I had put McDuff down. They came by after the service and wordlessly hugged and cried with me.

Monday morning found me back at work with eyes so swollen they looked like two slits. To be honest, I didn't think I had any more tears left in me. I was wrong.

My supervisor took one look at me and said, "Judy, you're in no condition to go into court. Why don't you go back home?"

Home without McDuff was the last place I wanted to go. All the strength I'd mustered to get dressed and go to work evaporated. I broke down crying and fled to my office in misery. I wanted to sink deeper into my pool of despair alone, but that didn't happen. Instead, something beautiful took place. My colleagues threw a lifeline that warmed my heart.

All day long, person after person came by to hug me, cry with me, and tell stories of dogs they'd lost. It amazed me how many of them sympathized, shared, and eased my grief on that sorrowful day.

Weeks passed. I concealed my anguish in public. It was a different story at night in the privacy of my bedroom. Night after night I shed tears for McDuff.

Early one morning, I heard barking outside my bedroom window. I knew the difference between the bark of a large or small dog. This one sounded huge. Since I lived in an apartment complex that limits size to thirty pounds, I wondered how anyone managed to sneak in such a big animal without being reported.

While I pondered it, I heard something that took my breath away. A bark I would know anywhere rang out and reverberated throughout the room.

McDuff barked twice from the floor at the foot of the bed. He always did that in response to any dog he heard outside. The room filled with an uncanny quietness. My heart leaped in my chest. Indescribable elation and joy surged through every part of my body as I screamed, "McDuff!"

I felt the bed sag under the weight of his body. He jumped onto it where he usually did, the bottom right side. Lying there in shock, unable to move, and barely breathing, I was conscious of the indentation of footprints walking along the side of the bed.

I felt the shape of that familiar head thrush up under my hand, the way he always did whenever he wanted me to pet him. Then, in an instant — poof. He was gone.

I didn't see him at any time, but I sensed his presence, felt the pressure of his paws walking on the side of my bed, and his furry head under my hand. Make no doubt about it, McDuff had been in the room with me that night.

Instead of experiencing sadness after he left the room, a feeling of ecstasy and happiness flooded through me like a raging river. From that moment on, the deep, debilitating grief disappeared. Oh, I still cried from time to time when something reminded me of him — I still do — but it was different. I knew he had come back to tell me, *Snap out of it. You know better than this. Stop feeling sorry for yourself and get on with your life* — and I did.

I've read that the bond between a therapy dog and its owner is stronger than the bond between other dogs and owners. I believe that's one reason I experienced such extreme, prolonged devastation at the end of his life.

McDuff didn't let death stop him from coming back to comfort me. Even after his life ended, he continued to provide his spirit dog therapy and love. Only this time, directed exclusively at me to lift me out of my sorrow and despair.

I didn't know it at the time, but he wasn't done. McDuff would continue on his mission to comfort others. Long after his death, he was still on the job.

## Never Again

Never again will I see those wise mystical eyes,
Eyes I loved so well, burn into mine;
Eyes that created joy and comfort,
Healing and calmness, amusement and laughter,
And tears of frustration.

Never again will I witness your tender tongue
Convey love and unconditional acceptance;
The tongue that brought smiles to the faces
Of the sick and disabled.

Never again will you be there to lick the tears
Away from my face, if ever life beats me
Down to the ground again.

Never again will I feel the comfort and protection
Of your furry back against my leg
As we lie sleeping in bed.

Forever more will I hold in my heart
The life lessons you taught,
How to forgive, love unconditionally,
Look beyond outer appearances,
Enjoy life instead of fighting and resisting it,
And to help myself by being of service to others.

Farewell, my teacher, my friend, my companion;
The joy and blessing of having you in my life
Far outweighed the pain of losing you.

Farewell, my McDuff, until we meet again,
And I gaze into those eyes once more.

—JUDY MCFADDEN

CHAPTER 16

# Good-byes for McDuff

*Don't be dismayed at goodbyes, a farewell is
necessary before you can meet again and meeting
again, after moments or lifetimes, is certain for
those who are friends.*
—RICHARD BACH

DARKNESS SURROUNDED US AS WE WALKED THROUGH THE PARKING
lot of Green Valley Ranch Casino. Steven's mood shifted
shortly after we left the buffet, becoming as dark as the night.
We got into the car and drove away with his brooding silence
engulfing us. The stillness shattered when an anguished question rang out in the car begging for an answer and finality.

"Judy, are you sure McDuff said it was alright?"

"Yes, he told me it was okay for me to put him down, Steven,"
I reassured him.

Grief-stricken, Steven had to accept that he would not see
his buddy again. There would be no more weekend sleepovers,
or reading books to him in the Reading with Rover Program,
or appearing on television programs together. Kids are resilient,
though. I knew he would bounce back from this heartache a
lot faster than I would.

The day I told Steven about putting McDuff down was
one of the harder things I've ever had to do. The drive to his
house earlier that evening filled me with dread. The moment

I walked in the door alone, Steven looked at me and asked, "Where's McDuff?"

I knew breaking the news to Steven would devastate him. I'd already talked it over with Susan, and she decided I should be the one to tell the kids.

"Steven, I've got something sad to tell you," I said. "I had to put McDuff down."

Susan had started tearing up the moment I walked in the door. Little Amy climbed into her mother's arms and held on tight as tears trickled down their cheeks. Steven looked at me, his eyes wide in disbelief, and then his body crumpled onto the sofa.

"McDuff was in a lot of pain from the cancer. The pain pills stopped helping him. I couldn't stand to see him suffer any longer," I continued as I sat down beside him. I held him in my arms as his shoulders shook from the sobs that wracked his body.

"Steven, McDuff let me know that it was okay. He was ready to go. And, there's something he wanted you to have to remember him by," I said, placing McDuff's beloved red leash in his hands.

He ran his hand over it and looked at me, his eyes swimming in tears. I knew what that leash had meant to McDuff and what it meant to me. It was my way of giving Steven a piece of McDuff to keep the memory of what they shared alive. I hated to part with it, but McDuff taught me to think of others instead of myself.

I handed Steven a photograph of McDuff. Calming down, he sat fingering the leash while he looked at the picture with sniffles shaking his body. Emotionally spent, all of us sat there not uttering a word.

"Steven, would you go with me to the buffet at Green Valley Ranch Casino? I've been too upset to eat much lately, and I need a good meal."

I'd already discussed it with Susan as we tried to think of something to take Steven's mind off McDuff's death. He hesitated for a while, and said, "Yes," in a quivering voice. I could tell his heart wasn't in it. He only agreed to please me.

We told Susan and Amy that we'd see them later and left the house. Neither of us spoke after we got into the car, too choked up to trust ourselves to say anything. The casino wasn't far from Steven's house. It didn't take us long to get there, and for a change, there wasn't a long line for the buffet.

While waiting to be seated, I tried to think of ways to cheer Steven up. I didn't have an appetite, but thought the fabulous variety of food might tempt the taste buds of a growing boy. Maybe, it would take his mind off what I'd told him. After we were led to our table, we went over to check out the culinary delights that awaited us.

We walked over to the serving area and breathed in the aromas of soups, vegetables, casseroles, and pizza. Sparkling from the escaping juices, the roasted chicken, beef, and ham on carving boards beckoned to us.

Pies, cakes, and an array of mouth-watering chocolate desserts seduced our nostrils. A variety of other tempting food completed the selection. Everything looked and smelled so good.

"Steven, look at the pizza, and there's so many desserts to choose from. What are you getting?" I said, attempting to interest him in the delicious assortment before him. We finally made our choices, returned to our table, sat down, and picked at our food. I could see that Steven was still troubled. *This is a good time to explain more in detail about McDuff*, I thought.

"Steven, McDuff communicated with me by looking deep into my eyes. He let me know he wanted to be put down. I couldn't stand to see him suffer any longer. After the veterinarian gave him the shot, it ended right away. It didn't hurt him."

Steven listened without saying a word as he pushed the food around on his plate with his fork. His rigid body posture softened. He began to eat the way only a growing boy can. Watching him, my appetite perked up, too. After a trip for seconds, we finished our desserts and left the buffet with stomachs filled to the brim.

I gave the thumbs up sign to Susan when I dropped him off. He would adjust to McDuff's absence, and he had Lucky to console him. Having McDuff around on weekends was instrumental in convincing Steven's parents to let him have a dog of his own. Now, one more person had to receive the news of McDuff's death. Telling Darlene would be every bit as hard as telling Steven.

Darlene was a heavy smoker and knew it wasn't good for her. She tried hard, but couldn't overcome her addiction to cigarettes. I noticed what started out as a slight cough became progressively worse.

She complained about feeling tired all the time, but contributed it to her age. Warning bells went off in my head. I kept encouraging her to see her doctor and get a chest X-ray. Finally, she agreed and went.

"Judy, I went back to the doctor today for the X-ray results. He says I have lung cancer," Darlene said in anguish.

Even though I wasn't surprised, it rattled me. I feared that at her age, and after years of heavy smoking, the prognosis would not be favorable. However, after completion of radiation therapy, the doctors pronounced her cancer in remission. Maybe she had beaten it after all.

During Darlene's radiation treatments, McDuff's visits had become therapy dog visits to his friend. He always brought joy to her, but now, even more so. She delighted in hearing the new places he visited, giving him treats, and spoiling him with toys.

Knowing how she felt about him, and after all she'd been through, telling her about putting McDuff down was the last thing I wanted to do. Stuck in an agonizing time warp, I relived his death over and over as I said those good-byes.

"Darlene, I have something to tell you. I'll be right over," I said over the phone. Her eyes searched mine as I entered the door. She knew the pills weren't working, and it hurt her to know that he suffered. No words were spoken. We embraced and cried together. She walked across the living room, picked up his picture, and cradled it in her arms.

"It's a blessing he didn't have to suffer any longer, Judy," she said with a faraway look on her face. *Was she wondering about what may be ahead for her?* I wondered. Would I have to face losing her, too?

"Judy, I've just come from the doctor's office. The lung cancer has returned," she said sadly about a year after McDuff's death. "My daughters want me to move to Portland, Oregon to be near them."

I'd miss Darlene, but I knew it was better for her to be near her family, especially for help with doctor visits and medical care. Sadness overwhelmed me after talking with her.

McDuff's mission ended on that Halloween morning in the vet's office and so did my journey with him. I thought my precious McDuff was gone forever, but that stubborn Scottie stayed on the job.

# Still on the Job

*We only live once, but once is enough*
*if we do it right. Live your life with class, dignity,*
*and style so that an exclamation,*
*rather than a question mark signifies it!*
—GARY RYAN BLAIR

THE NOVEMBER 28, 2001 *ANTHEM VIEW* FRONT PAGE, WITH A PHOTO of McDuff and one of the clients at Project PRIDE, informed its readers: "MCDUFF IS ON THE JOB."

After his life ended on October 31, 2003, Steven, his mother, the staff at the Paseo Verde Library, Darlene, and I thought those words no longer applied. We were all wrong. I found out from the card on flowers sent to me that he did indeed remain on the job.

Sympathy cards and phone calls poured in from friends across the country after they learned of McDuff's death. One afternoon I heard a knock at the door and opened it to see a man standing there with a glass vase filled with flowers.

The magnificent floral arrangement was huge. *One of my friends knew flowers would cheer me up,* I thought while placing them on the fireplace mantle. I drank in the beauty and sweet fragrance of the multi-colored roses, chrysanthemums, marigolds, daisies, and a variety of other flowers, and wondered who had sent them.

I tore open the attached card and read, "Thinking of you. I know how much you are loved. McDuff." *That can't be right. It's signed by McDuff. I must have read it wrong.* Looking at it again, I still couldn't believe my eyes.

I searched the card for the florist's phone number and called. "I received flowers from your shop, and there must be some mistake," I told the lady who answered. "The card has a message from McDuff. That can't be correct. That's the name of the dog that I had put down. Can you give me an explanation?"

"I'm so sorry for the mix up," she answered. "I know what you are going through, because I had my dog put down a few months ago. I feel awful about this. Let me make some calls and get right back to you."

She called back after several minutes and said, "The flowers are from Linda Peck. The card should have read, 'Thinking of you. I know how much you loved McDuff.' The signature should have been Linda Peck and not McDuff. Nothing like this has ever happened before. I can't tell you how sorry I am."

Half an hour later, another arrangement of flowers arrived from the florist with an apology. She had no way of knowing about the exceptional dog involved, and that he would return to me after his death to snap me out of my intense grief. McDuff reached out to comfort me through the one thing that never failed to lift my spirits — flowers.

That was just the beginning. He had work to do with others, and it continued at the Paseo Verde Library. I received a call from Steven's mother the February after McDuff's death.

"Judy, Steven and I were asked by the Paseo Verde Library to participate in taping for a DVD presentation to highlight the Reading with Rover Program. Senator Reid nominated the library to participate in a national library competition. Can you come?"

"I'd love to. I'll see if I can leave work early."

Hurrying to the parking garage from the courthouse, I worried about getting to the library late. The horrific traffic situation in Las Vegas defies description, and this day proved no different. When I finally walked into the reading room where I'd spent so many Saturday mornings with McDuff and Steven, the taping was in progress.

A peculiar sight caught my eye as I entered the door. Florica and several library employees stood in a line passing a box of tissue from one to the other. I drew closer. *What's going on here?* I thought as I saw faces with tears streaming down.

Tissue after tissue was plucked from the box as it made its way up and down the line. Something had stirred and touched them to the core, but what?

A bright light shone directly on Steven and his mother, and a man focused the camera on them. The turmoil I witnessed was caused by the taping taking place on the other side of the room.

I listened as Susan spoke of how Steven was chosen to be one of the first four participants in the library's Reading with Rover Program, and the bond that developed among Steven, his family, McDuff, and me.

She told how Steven's grades went from D average to As within two sessions. How his self-esteem soared when he made the honor roll for the first time. She expressed her gratitude to McDuff, me, and the Henderson District Public Library system for introducing the program.

Steven had been sitting quietly beside his mother as she talked, his emotions bubbling beneath the surface. He began to speak in a low hesitating voice, but gained volume and strength as he went along. You could feel his pain as he talked about McDuff.

As the box of tissues flew by me on another round, I understood for the first time how much of an impact McDuff had made in his life and in the lives of others.

A book in a display beside Steven and Susan with two dogs on the cover caught my attention during the filming. Afterward, Florica picked up the children's book, *McDuff Goes to School*, by Rosemary Wells, and asked me to read the dedication from the library.

"In Loving Memory of McDUFF — A wonderful Reading with Rover canine buddy and incredible therapy dog friend.

You will always have a special place in the heart of Henderson District Public Libraries and its children."

The book dedicated to him bore witness to his legacy. So overcome with emotion, I couldn't speak, I hugged Florica instead. My spirits soared as I left the library. McDuff would be remembered by Paseo Verde Library even though he no longer inhabits this earth. Through others, McDuff reached out and touched me that day. But, he wasn't finished. A strange incident happened after we left the library.

Susan invited me to stop by her house nearby. I left the parking lot first with Steven riding with me. Susan and Amy left later in Susan's car. Stopping at a stop sign near Susan's house, I beheld a sight that caused me to do a double take.

A man with a Scottish terrier that looked exactly like McDuff — the same size and the same color — stood waiting to cross the street. It surprised me to see a Scottie, because they're rarely seen out here in the desert.

Steven and I watched him, transfixed. The dog caught my eye and stared without wavering, the way McDuff did. I felt a connection to McDuff through him and a wonderful sense of peace and joy came over me as we pulled away.

"Steven, I wonder if your mom and Amy are coming this way. If they go the other way to your house, they'll miss the Scottie," I said. We pulled into the driveway. Shortly after, Susan and Amy pulled in behind us. I didn't have to ask. I could see it on their faces. "Did you see him?" Susan shrieked as she jumped out of her car.

We went inside and shared our experiences. Susan told me the Scottie held her gaze, too. "I've never seen anyone walking a Scottie around here before, and I do my fair share of driving," Susan told me.

The library taping had been a mixed bag for all of us. On one hand it brought pleasure, but on the other hand, it dug up buried pain — like peeling the scab from a healing wound. Seeing that Scottie after we left the library uplifted all of us, and we agreed it wasn't a coincidence. Next, McDuff turned to his friend, Darlene, to comfort her in the last days of her life.

I received a Christmas card in 2005 from Darlene that did not bear tidings of great joy. Her doctor advised the lung cancer was terminal, and that she didn't have long to live. A new chemotherapy treatment might give her a little more time, and she agreed to it.

She wrote she had no fear of dying, that she knew where she was going, and that she was in God's hands. Her wish to spend her last Christmas with her sons and daughters became a reality when they all arrived for the holidays. Then, I read something that sent chills up and down my spine and brought tears to my eyes.

"I keep McDuff's picture in front of me and just know he is in my arms comforting me and tears fall. Maybe I will see him soon."

With a lump in my throat, I read it again. Incredibly, McDuff still provided comfort to Darlene long after his death. Looking at his picture helped her face her approaching death. His spirit dog journey started when I picked him up and held him at the age of eight-weeks-old, and it never seemed to end.

On that day at the kennel when I first held McDuff in the palm of my hand and stared into those dark eyes and heard, *I wonder what adventures we two are going to have together,* I knew he was extraordinary. Intelligence is a characteristic of the terrier breed, but his soared off the charts. It wasn't a coincidence when he sat on the black slipper to hide it from me.

Obedience training saw him surpass every dog in his class to claim not only the trophy, but the first place blue ribbon as well. His instructor gave him the highest score in her years of training dogs.

The TDI evaluator saluted his superiority when he remarked, "That Scottish terrier is something else." And, more than once, McDuff frustrated and outsmarted me — remember the pill battle?

One of my neighbors saw me walking him one day and started a conversation. As we walked away, he said, "I'm going to call him 'The Professor.'" I didn't have to ask why. Attitude and dignity oozed from him.

He refused to shake hands or learn tricks. He wouldn't carry a baton in his mouth in agility class, or wear frivolous hats. He didn't have time for silliness. McDuff had a mission to complete.

When he began therapy dog work, his uniqueness became even more obvious. I knew something extraordinary existed in the way he connected with people and animals. He attracted unusual interest and enthusiasm wherever I took him.

I can't tell you how many times someone said to me, "Is that a Scottish terrier?" Children ran up exclaiming, "I've got him on my sweater," or on some other article in their possession.

My friends at the law firm begged me for "McDuff stories." He provided a never-ending supply. The way he connected with people is one of the reasons I decided to write a book about him. Down through the years, he formed close bonds with my dearest friends. Sure, I've admired and liked other people's dogs, but I've never loved someone else's dog the way they loved McDuff.

Trudy, Darlene, Steven and his family, Minnie, and the disabled residents at Opportunity Village's Project PRIDE truly loved McDuff, and he loved them right back. He belonged to them as much as he belonged to me. Possessiveness was out of the question for me.

I shared McDuff whether I liked it or not. Everyone wanted him. I soon learned he didn't belong to me, and he wanted it that way. He loved sleepovers at Steven's house, staying with Minnie during my mother's trial, and visiting and boarding with his veterinarians — no separation anxiety for my dog.

Dragging him, resisting all the way, through the parking lot to my car at the Opportunity Village Henderson campus left no doubt in my mind where he'd rather stay. That's not to say he didn't love me and that we weren't extremely close.

An uncanny telepathy existed between us from the beginning. We knew each other's thoughts. Now, I understand why training him was so easy. He received mentally what I wanted him to do, and he did it — when he wanted to. It happened so naturally that I didn't realize what was taking place.

When I said to Steven that McDuff let me know it was okay to put him down, I told the truth. I listened to him and learned from him in the years we spent together.

Anyone can relate to the lessons McDuff taught, whether Christian, Jew, Buddhist, Shintoist, any other religion, or no religion at all. Young and old, people of all races and cultures can learn something from him about life and living.

McDuff taught about unconditional love, forgiveness, looking beyond appearances, nonresistance, and being of service to others — important lessons for anyone.

He loved everybody and everything, even cats, supposedly his natural enemy. The things he disliked or that annoyed him, birds, monkeys, squirrels, and most of all the UPS truck, wouldn't have been harmed if he caught them. The thrill for him was in the chase. Forgiveness and not holding a grudge came naturally to McDuff. Those were the hardest lessons for me to learn, but learn them I did. Clinging to negative emotions and reliving unpleasant experiences hurt me more than anyone else involved. I've moved on without bitterness or hard feelings toward my ex-husband regarding the nasty divorce and domestic violence.

I forgive the man responsible for my mother's death. I don't feel vindictive or derive any pleasure from thinking of him in prison. He repaid kindness with violence and larceny, and he is paying the price. That's the way it goes. You get back what you send out in life, good or bad; you reap what you sow.

When I first walked into the room at Project PRIDE, I saw severely impaired individuals and couldn't wait to get away from them. But, McDuff looked beyond the damaged, imperfect bodies and minds, and went to work comforting and loving them.

He delved below the surface and made a connection deep within them, and by doing that, he taught me an important lesson — not to judge others by appearances.

Nonresistance and turning the other cheek are hard for most of us. Although Scottish terriers are known for their aggressive and combative temperament, McDuff chose to go the other way. He didn't challenge or fight the pit bull that attacked him. Instead, he weathered the storm, stood up, shook it off, and walked away. He never looked back. I've learned to do that, too.

McDuff's therapy dog work really opened my eyes. He didn't expect any return or reward for his service, and served eagerly and willingly. McDuff did all the work. I was just his chauffeur along for the ride, but I gained much on the journey with him.

My therapy dog volunteer work taught me that by helping others, I helped myself. Nothing makes a person feel better, or chases away loneliness and self-pity, more than taking time to be of service to others.

It's not hard to sit down and listen to a child read a book, or visit a nursing home or hospital with your dog. Children's lives and futures can be changed by sitting in a room and reading to your dog.

Many elderly, lonely and neglected nursing home residents would benefit and be grateful to you for your time. What better way for a church member to put a smile on the face of the sick, shut-in, or hospitalized than to bring a furry friend along during a visit? The smile on their face is worth the time and effort.

Now that McDuff is gone, my therapy dog volunteer days are over, but his example of serving others stays with me. I volunteer every week at the front desk of St. Rose Dominican Hospitals, Rose de Lima Campus, where he made his therapy dog visits. McDuff taught me well.

I hope this book will inspire you to volunteer with your dogs in organizations like TDI or Reading with Rover — especially retirees and baby boomers looking for something worthwhile to do with their spare time. I promise, it will change and fulfill your lives the way it did mine.

*Eight-week-old McDuff on Christmas Day, 1994. Check out that bow.*

*My maternal great-grandmother, Jennie Sawyers, whose mother was a Chippewa Indian and father a Scotch-Irish Virginia horse breeder.*

*A Scottie with attitude and long, long ears.*

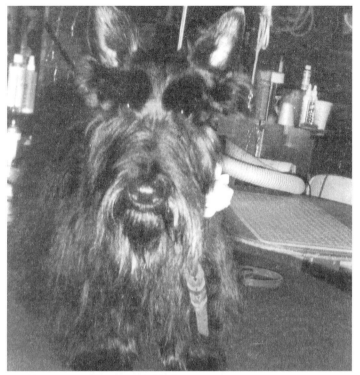

*Spiffy therapy dog McDuff after grooming.*

*McDuff in chair where domestic violence incident occurred.*

*My son, Kelly, and McDuff.*

*My friend, Linda Peck, and her Japanese Chins.*

*My friend, Marie Parks, and me in Paris.*

*Should I sneak upstairs and steal something?*

*McDuff and me while he was still fairly small.*

*Where does she think she's going in those boots?*

*My friend, Trudy Knight, and me at going away party.*

*Jennie, McDuff's Scottie buddy, and Santa Claus.*

*Steven, McDuff, and McDuff's beloved red leash.*

*Steven & McDuff in Children's Library Reading Room.*

*McDuff, the Therapy Dog.*

*Sleepovers at Steven's house.*

In Loving Memory of
**McDUFF**
A Wonderful *Reading With Rover*
canine buddy and incredible therapy dog
friend.  You will always have a special
place in the heart of
Henderson District Public Libraries
and its children.

Henderson District Public Libraries

*Dedication page of book at the Paseo Verde Library.*

*Florica Hagendorn, Henderson Libraries' Reading with Rover Coordinator, and her boxers.*

# Epilogue

*Are you bored with life? Then throw yourself into some work you believe in with all your heart, live for it, die for it, and you will find happiness that you had thought could never be yours.*

—DALE CARNEGIE

STEVEN IS IN THE 10TH GRADE AT CORONADO HIGH SCHOOL IN Henderson, Nevada. His mother tells me he is a big reader and doing well in school — making As in advanced science class. He scored in the 75th percentile nationwide for reading comprehension on the Iowa Tests. Steven wants to become a veterinarian. Wouldn't McDuff love that!

Opportunity Village's Project PRIDE expanded since McDuff and I first visited Chris, Nathaniel, Naomi, Matthew, and Kathy in 2001. The program now administers to over 35 people with severe intellectual and physical disabilities, and has a long waiting list.

Opportunity Village serves 720 people with intellectual disabilities every day, and many of those individuals work in the community. By telling the story of McDuff and his devotion to the clients at Project PRIDE, perhaps, readers will institute programs like it in their states.

TDI is the oldest registry of therapy dogs in the United States, but there are similar organizations across the country. Certified therapy dogs provide emotional service, unlike service dogs that assist people with disabilities.

K9 Advantix® sponsors the AKC Canine Good Citizen Test used to evaluate temperament and determine suitability for therapy dog certification. Dogs must be at least one-year-old, can be any size, but do not have to be purebred. Shelter and rescue dogs are used with excellent results.

I became affiliated with Reading with Rover through the Paseo Verde Library in Henderson, Nevada. What began with McDuff and three other dogs now fluctuates between eight to twenty dogs and volunteers.

A special Children's Literacy room is designated at the Library for children to read to therapy dogs. If your child has reading difficulties that are affecting school work, talk to the teacher at school about Reading with Rover or similar programs.

Vorys, Sater, Seymour and Pease grew from a four-story building in Columbus to offices in Cleveland, Cincinnati, and Akron, Ohio, Washington, D.C., Alexandria, Virginia, and Houston, Texas.

Many of my friends still work there and keep in touch with me. E-mail and unlimited cell phone minutes are a boon to long-distance relationships. We share deaths, births, illnesses, and snow covered yards from across the miles.

Kelly remains my best friend, rock, and foundation. If he weren't my son, I'd still like, admire, and respect him. He's the biggest blessing and pride of my life. I look forward to our yearly one-week vacation that is our way of making up for the time apart after he moved back to Ohio.

Years have passed since I put McDuff down. Some of my friends told me to get another dog right away. Others said to wait until I stopped hurting. I told them I could never find another dog to replace McDuff. They thought I felt that way because of my grief. That wasn't it at all. I knew I'd expect way too much from a new dog, and that wouldn't be fair.

Any newcomer would probably place somewhere in the middle at obedience school graduation, eagerly learn tricks like shaking hands, and eat as soon as I put food in its dog dish. It would come every time I wanted to pet it, greet me with unbridled joy each time I came in the door, and never stray far from my side.

Taking pills when sick, refraining from rolling in unsavory substances, and playing with, instead of destroying, toys would be easy things for it to do. It would hate cats, pit bulls, and going to the veterinarian. And do you know something? That kind of dog would bore me silly after McDuff.

The poor new canine couldn't outsmart me, or communicate with me through telepathy. Understanding how to comfort the dying, sick, elderly, or a lonely childless widow would prove far too complicated for it. Connecting with terribly disabled individuals, boosting a schoolboy's self-esteem, or soothing frightened ducklings would be out of its league. I'd be so disappointed in the poor creature.

What life lessons could it teach me more important than how to love unconditionally, forgive those who harm you, look beyond outer appearances to the inside of others, and enjoy life instead of fighting and resisting it? Could it teach how to want to help and serve others wholeheartedly?

No more dogs for me. I am content to pass on McDuff's legacy through this book. If just one person becomes inspired to volunteer with their dog and/or start up a therapy dog or animal assisted reading program, I'll be satisfied. Through that person I'll know that McDuff is still on the job.

I look back over my life on the mission with McDuff and see what came out of the times of heartache and tribulation — a much stronger and spiritual person. I know that everything happens for good if you learn from and grow through the negative experiences in life.

Faith in a higher power, my son, old friends, and a stubborn hilarious Scottish terrier got me through some rough spots. Even though my heart broke when I lost him, I knew he had changed my life forever. As long as I remember to live by the lessons he taught, McDuff will always be with me.

## No Other Way

Could we but see the pattern of our days,
We should discern how devious were the ways
By which we came to this, the present time,
This place in life; and we should see the climb
Our soul has made up through the years.
We should forget the hurts, the wanderings, the fears,
The wastelands of our life and know
That we could come no other way or grow
Into our good without these steps our feet
Found hard to take, our faith found hard to meet.
The road of life winds on, and we like travelers go
From turn to turn until we come to know
The truth that life is endless and that we
Forever are inhabitants of all eternity.

— MARTHA SMOCK

## Contact Information

Readers can contact the following for information on therapy dog, animal assisted reading, and community rehabilitation programs:

**Therapy Dogs International**
88 Bartley Road
Flanders, New Jersey 07836
Phone: (973) 252-9800
E-mail: tdi@gti.net
Website: www.tdi-dog.org

**American Kennel Club**
**Canine Good Citizen Department**
PO Box 900064
Raleigh, North Carolina 27675-9064
Phone: (919) 816-3894
E-mail: cgc@akc.org
Website: www.akc.org

**Henderson Libraries Reading with Rover**
Florica Hagendorn
Reading with Rover Coordinator
280 South Green Valley Parkway
Henderson, Nevada 89012
Phone: (702) 492-6586
Website: www.mypubliclibrary.com

**Opportunity Village**
6300 West Oakey Blvd.
Las Vegas, Nevada 89146
Phone: (702) 259-3700
Website: www.opportunityvillage.org

## Ordering Information

Visit *www.lifewithmcduff.com*, or *www.bookmasters.com*, or
call **800-247-6553** to order additional copies
or for bulk orders of *Life With McDuff.*

Contact Judy McFadden to arrange a speaking engagement
at: *www.lifewithmcduff.com.*

If this book has impacted your life, or you have volunteered
with therapy dogs, or animal assisted reading programs,
we would like to hear from you. Please contact us at:
*summit86mountainpub@yahoo.com*

or write to us at:

Summit Mountain Publishing

PO Box 91528
Henderson, NV 89009-1528